Treasures
of the
Louvre

Alain Nave

Treasures of the Louvre

Translated by Rosalie Gomes

BARNES
& NOBLE
BOOKS

NEW YORK

The history of the Louvre spans eight centuries, from its early days as a fortress under Philippe Auguste to the inauguration of the 'largest museum in the world'. During that time, the Louvre has never ceased to be an affair of State. The Chinese-American architect I.M. Pei, who was entrusted in 1983 with the project of transforming the Louvre into the Grand Louvre, succinctly described the complexity of the task: 'It's a museum, a palace, and a monument.'

Monuments are often preserved, along with their successive strata. This can lead to their petrification, ruling out new uses of the structure. Palaces too are preserved, and their architecture and successive decorations maintained for visitors. But, just as Lot's wife was changed to stone because she looked backwards towards Sodom, so palaces too may become frozen if they only look to the past. The museum's task is to display exhibits, but to do so it needs the consent of the monument and the palace.

For many years, respect for the historical building resulted in stagnation. If the Louvre is now once more a living space, it is doubtless because the Grand Louvre successfully combines the monument-palace-museum trinity in its structure as an essential prerequisite.

The monument has now been restored in its entirety, while respecting its surrounding environment. From the Cour Carrée to the Place de la Concorde, it follows the slight curve of the Seine, and offers the viewer the most majestic perspective in the world. As Ieoh Ming Pei has said: 'All great ideas are simple.' This perspective is punctuated by simple geometric forms: the square shape of the Louvre's first courtyard, the pyramid, the arc of the Arc du Carrousel, the Obelisk in the Place de la Concorde, followed by another arc –the Arc de Triomphe– and, in the distance, the massive yet airy cube of the Arche de la Défense. The museum exists without harming the palace. The summer apartments, embellished by Anne of Austria's painted stucco ornamentation, now house the collections of Roman sculpture: the juxtaposition makes us more aware of the 17th century's love for Antiquity. Since the list of such fruitful exchanges between the works of art and their surroundings is long, let us cite just a few examples: the gallery of the Caryatids, the Grande Galerie, the 'Egyptian museum' housed in Charles X's rooms, the rooms of the Duc de Morny. The latter offers the viewer a final glance at the works of the Second Empire, now mainly housed at the Musée d'Orsay; it also fulfilled Henri IV's dream of linking the Palais du Louvre with the Palais des Tuileries.

The history of the Louvre is the history of its collections, which ultimately reveal the taste and sensitivity of the collectors. Following the Revolution, the history of the Louvre became the history of the museum at a time when a more encyclopaedic perception of its cultural role was developing: the museum's function was now to illustrate the culture of a time or of a country while disregarding questions of hierarchy.

The Grand Louvre is a space of surprising juxtapositions in which taste and learning meet, just as they did during the Renaissance, when Pierre Lescot built the Louvre's first façade.

Frontispiece

Equestrian statue of Louis XIV, in the Cour Napoleon

Lead copy of an equestrian statue of Louis XIV, executed by Bernini in 1674 and transformed by François Girardon in 1687 into a statue of 'Marcus Curtius throwing himself into the flames'. The transformation was accepted by the king because he had been disappointed with Bernini's work, as the Marquis de Dangeau recorded in his diary: 'Wednesday 14 [November 1685], Versailles. – The King was wandering through the Orangery, which he found to be wonderfully magnificent; then he saw Chevalier Bernini's equestrian statue that had been placed there, and he felt that the man and the horse were so poorly executed that he decided not only to have the statue removed, but also to have it destroyed.'

Originally published as *The Grand Louvre* by Editions Adam Biro, 1997
Copyright © 1997 by Société nouvelle Adam Biro
English translation by Rosalie Gomes
This edition published by Barnes & Noble, Inc., by arrangement with Editions Adam Biro, Paris
1998 Barnes & Noble Books
ISBN 0-7607-1067-8
Printed and bound in China
04 05 06 07 M 9 8 7 6 5 4

Eight Centuries
of History

By the end of the 12th century, the city of Paris had grown beyond the confines of the Ile de la Cité, the original civitas, where the royal palace stood and the cathedral of Notre Dame was being built. A new urban centre was spreading from Les Halles to the slopes of the Montagne Sainte Geneviève. The king was about to set out on a Crusade, and something had to be done to protect the newly expanded city.

The fortress outside the ramparts

Beginning on the Right Bank in 1190, Philippe Auguste built a rampart around the growing city. The wall took in the settlements on both banks of the Seine as well as the outlying quarters, and its construction was completed twenty years later. The new ramparts encouraged the growth of Paris inside the city walls. A sign of prestige for a rising power, the wall also served as a symbol of the city's –and the kingdom's– impregnability. In the short term, the erection of the ramparts was justified by the reigning climate of political hostility between France and the Normans in the British Isles. Paris had to be protected, especially on the vulnerable downstream part of the Seine. To strengthen the city's defences, a fortress was erected outside the western wall on the banks of the Seine and named 'Le Louvre' after the site on which it was constructed. Though the origin of the name remains obscure, 'Louvre' is thought to derive from the Latin Lupara, meaning a dog used to hunt wolves. Begun in 1190, the original Louvre was completed in 1202. Though it benefitted from recent developments in military architecture, Louis Philippe's Louvre was nevertheless built according to the principles of classical strongholds. The moat-ringed ramparts enclosed a rectangle with nearly equal long and short sides. A tower stood at each right angle, and twin towers guarded each of the two gateways –one facing the Seine, the other facing the city to the east.

The dungeon, known as 'La Grosse Tour' (Big Tower), stood in the courtyard and was surrounded by a dry ditch. Of the buildings constructed against the southern, or riverside, ramparts and the western wall, only the Salle Saint Louis still stands today. The fortress, which served first as an arsenal and later as a prison, was deemed an unsafe place to store the royal treasury in 1297.

From stronghold to royal residence

In 1358, the merchants' provost, Étienne Marcel, called for the strengthening of the defences of Paris, especially in areas whose population had grown significantly. A new rampart was erected on the Right Bank, stretching from the Porte Sainte Antoine (where Charles V, also known as Charles the Wise, was constructing the Bastille) to the Porte Saint Denis. It then traveled southward till it reached the Seine, where it followed the riverbank a scant few hundred yards from the Louvre before meeting up with Philippe Auguste's earlier rampart. Since the fortress was now located inside the city, it no longer played a truly defensive role. In 1360, Charles V entrusted Raymond du Temple with the task of transforming the fortress into a royal residence. Two new wings were built, on the northern and eastern sides, and the 'curtains' (the part of a wall connecting two bastions or towers) were raised and terraced. To facilitate access to the upper floors, several spiral staircases were constructed, and turrets were added to the towers. The façades were pierced with mullioned windows. To house the sovereign and his court, apartments were created and embellished, and new accommodations were built. The decorative arts were not forgotten: adornments included statues and wall carvings, and, on the pepperbox turrets, golden weathercocks and finials. This is how the new château was depicted on one of the pages of the illuminated manuscript *The Very Rich Hours of the Duc de Berry*.

This ambitious venture failed, however, to keep France's wandering and sometimes martial monarchs at home in their royal dwelling, and even when they were in Paris, they often preferred to reside in the Hôtel Saint Pol or the Hôtel des Tournelles. But the main rival for royal affections was the peaceful Loire Valley, with 'its emerald banks, its vineyard-covered hills, its wheaten plains'. For more than a century, the forsaken Château du Louvre reverted to its original function as an arsenal and a prison.

From François I's Louvre to Catherine de' Medici's Tuileries

In a letter written in 1527 and addressed to his aldermen, François I expressed his desire to live in Paris: 'Conscious that we shall be more comfortably and more appropriately lodged in our castle at the Louvre, for such reason have we decided to have the aforementioned castle repaired and put in good order.' Recently released from captivity following the disastrous defeat at Pavia, François I now hoped to turn

Remains of the dungeon and moat of the medieval Louvre.

Preceding pages
The western wing of the Cour Carrée, showing the reverse side of Perrault's colonnade.

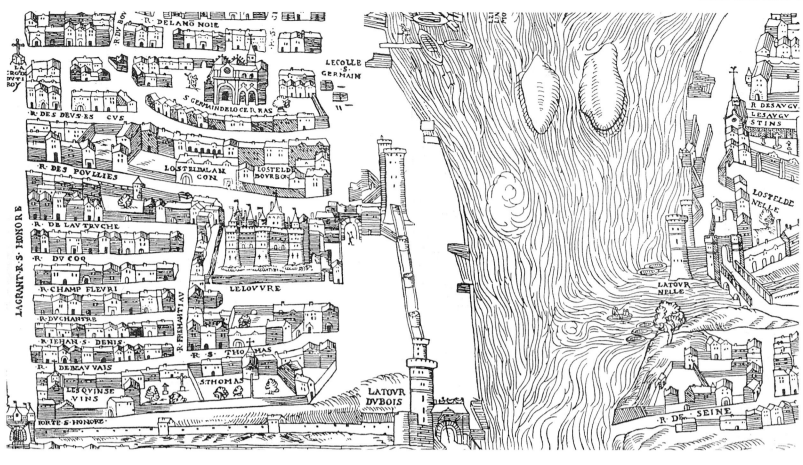

Charles V's castle into a fitting residence for the kings of France. First, the Grosse Tour was demolished and new outbuildings erected; then the existing apartments were rearranged, refurbished, and redecorated, and the windows enlarged. Outside the grounds, on the tow-paths on the banks of the Seine, workers began constructing quays and erecting the Porte Neuve, which became one of the gateways into Paris. In many respects, however, the Louvre remained a medieval stronghold. Two decades later, François I decided to further transform the Louvre into a palace more in tune with the spirit of the Renaissance. In 1546, Pierre Lescot was named to direct the renovation of the Louvre; he would be assisted by Jean Goujon, who was in charge of ornamental carvings and sculpture. When the king died the following year, his successor Henri II ordered Lescot to carry on the renovation. In Ronsard's words, addressed to Lescot: 'The sceptre is now held by Henri II, who of your valour [has] perfect knowledge.' Pierre Lescot demolished the fortress's western wing, replacing it with a two-storey building topped with an attic and trussed roof. At the far end of the building facing the Seine, he erected the Pavillon du Roi to house the sovereign's apartments. The luxurious interior decoration of Lescot's building included, on the ground floor, the Salle des Caryatides, whose name refers to the sculptures Goujon had copied from ancient Greek and Roman caryatids. Facing it was the small Salle du Tribunal, which was not, as its name implies, a court of law, but a separate gallery where the king sat when attending recep-

tions and festivities. The Salle des Gardes and the king's apartments were on the upper floor.

Henri II's untimely death in 1559 during a tournament did not put a stop to the renovation of the Louvre. Lescot was now commissioned to build a new wing facing the Seine to replace the old southern wall. It would not be completed until the reign of Henri IV. When Pierre Lescot died in 1578, the building he bequeathed to the nation was a remarkable fusion of classicism and traditional French architecture, according to the historian Anthony Blunt. Favouring the ornamental over the monumental, Lescot created a new style and contributed significantly to the definition of the characteristics of French Renaissance architecture. Lescot's Louvre was still under construction when the queen regent, Catherine de' Medici, decided that it was too small to house the court. When the young king came of age, Catherine, who wished to remain 'invisible but present', ordered Philibert De l'Orme to construct a new palace –the Tuileries– on the site of a former tilery (tuilerie, in French), just outside the ramparts built by Charles V and facing the Louvre. Catherine, ever invisible-but-present, then declared that she wished to connect both buildings with a long gallery built along the Seine, thus closing the imposing square formed by the two buildings. This may explain why her son Charles IX built the Petite Galerie near the Pavillon du Roi, on the site of an old canal that had connected the Seine with the moat of the medieval Louvre. The Petite Galerie would have served as the link between the Grande Galerie and the Louvre.

Map by Truchet

1551 (detail)

Despite the date, the map depicts the Louvre as it was during the reign of Charles V, not François I. In 1551, the Grosse Tour (Big Tower) had already been demolished, and the western wing of the castle replaced by Lescot's building. The map shows the quays, constructed by François I, as well as heavy urbanisation along the banks of the Seine. In case of an outside threat from the north of the rampart, a chain could be stretched across the Seine from the Tour du Coin to the facing Tour de Nesle.

10

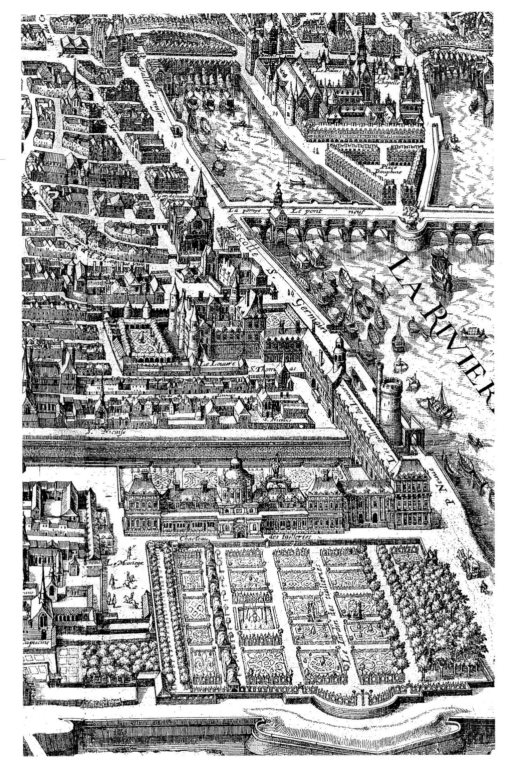

Map by Mérian

1615 (detail)

Several additions have been
made since Truchet's
earlier map, including
the Tuileries palace with
its landscaped gardens.
Charles V's rampart is still
visible between the two
palaces, connected by the
Grande Galerie. Both
wings of the Louvre and
the Pavillon du Roi,
constructed by Lescot,
are clearly visible.

proceeded to Notre Dame, where the Te Deum was sung in thanksgiving. It had taken him five years to consolidate his power and become king of a united France. If he was to rule the nation from the Louvre, the buildings would have to be equal to his political ambitions: they would have to be redesigned on a grand scale that went beyond the scope of Catherine de' Medici's earlier plans.

The result was the 'Grand Design', which called for the demolition of every vestige of the medieval castle and the connection of the Louvre with the Tuileries palace by two lateral galleries, located on the north and south sides.

In 1595, an additional floor was added to Charles IX's Petite Galerie. The construction of the 460-metre (503-yard) Grande Galerie, also known as the riverside gallery, was begun the same year. It would eventually link the Louvre with the Pavillon de Flore at the far end of the Tuileries. The eastern part of the gallery, located within Charles V's ramparts, was built by Louis Métezeau and still stands today. The western part, located outside the ramparts, was originally built by Jacques II Androuet Du Cerceau but was entirely reconstructed by Hector Lefuel in the 1850's. At first, the gallery was simply used as a covered passageway and reception area, but by the end of the 17th century it also housed the king's collection of scale models of fortified towns.

The gallery was sometimes put to strange uses: Henri IV once entertained the young Dauphin by holding a fox hunt there, and on another occasion, a camel, a present from the Duke of Nevers, was allowed to race through the gallery, to the great amusement of the future King Louis XIII!

In 1610, the Pavillon de Flore was covered, completing the construction of the Grande Galerie. Later that year, however, Henri IV was stabbed in Paris's Rue de la Ferronerie; he expired shortly afterwards at the Louvre, leaving his 'Grand Design' unfinished.

From Le Mercier's wing to Perrault's colonnade

If a political history of the Louvre were to be written, the thirty-year period covering the Regency and the reign of Louis XIII would doubtless fill a good portion of the book. During the Regency, Henri IV's 'Grand Design' was trimmed back, and no action was taken on it until 1624, when Louis XIII undertook the quadrupling of the size of the Cour Carrée –a project that Henri II had already envisaged. The western side of the courtyard was extended by the architect Jacques Le Mercier, who added new construction and prolonged Lescot's earlier building with the Pavillon de l'Horloge (also known as the Pavillon de Sully). The result was the Lescot-Le Mercier wing, still standing today.

When Philibert De l'Orme died, he was succeeded at the Tuileries by Jean Bullant. But work on the site was interrupted in 1572 –the year of the Saint Bartholomew's Day Massacre– when Catherine decided to embark on the construction of yet another residence. The Louvre, having witnessed the bloody Wars of Religion as well as countless festivities, would be abandoned once more when Henri III was forced to flee Paris.

Henri IV and his unfinished 'Grand Design'

In March 1594, Henri IV entered Paris through the Porte Neuve, which stood by the Seine next to the Louvre. He then

Le Mercier demolished the northern façade of the medieval castle and began new construction that was later stopped due to lack of funds.

In 1641, the painter Nicolas Poussin was commissioned to decorate the Grande Galerie with scenes from the life of Hercules. The project was never completed, and Poussin, fed up with the in-fighting at court, returned to Rome at the end of the following year. In 1643, at the time of Louis XIII's death, Anne of Austria and her son moved into the Palais Cardinal –the future Palais Royale. At the Louvre, the construction site remained closed.

Nine years later, on 21 October 1652, the young Louis XIV made a triumphant entry into Paris, putting an end to the years of social and political unrest known as the Fronde that had marked his childhood. 'Nearly everyone in the city as far as Saint Cloud came out to greet [him],' wrote Chancellor Le Tellier. Louis XIV moved into the Louvre and immediately ordered the refurbishing of the apartments under the direction of Le Mercier, who was succeeded by Le Vau in 1654. The murals painted by Romanelli on the vaults between Michel Anguier's stucco decorations in the queen mother's bedroom –which may still be seen on the ground floor of the Petite Galerie– date from this period. In 1659, a major new phase of construction was undertaken; it was of such a scale that it justified the publication of a decree prohibiting anyone from undertaking any type of building construction 'so as not to delay the service nor His Majesty's pleasure'. The new Louvre was to be the work of three key craftsmen whose work and complementary talents Louis XIV had already seen and admired at Vaux-le-Vicomte: the architect Louis Le Vau, the painter Charles Le Brun, and the landscape architect Le Nôtre. While the Louvre was being refurbished, the king would temporarily reside in the Tuileries palace, which Le Vau completed in record time, while Le Nôtre created an opulent backdrop of formal French gardens. Then Le Vau turned his attention to the construction of the northern wing of the Louvre (bordering today's Rue de Rivoli), following Le Mercier's plans. In 1661, he was commissioned to redo the first floor of the Petite Galerie, which had been destroyed by a fire, and profited from the occasion to extend the building. The interior decoration of the first floor gallery, named Galerie Apollon, was entrusted to Le Brun. But the unhurried pace of the work, which remained unfinished, provides evidence that Louis XIV was by then more interested in Versailles. Also in 1661, on the Seine side, Le Vau demolished part of the Hôtel du Petit-Bourbon, which had become an annex of the Louvre, in order to complete the wing begun by Lescot and construct a central pavilion. At the same time, the indefatigable Le Vau undertook the construction of the College of Four Nations (today's Institut de France) on the former site of the Tour de Nesle, facing the Louvre on the opposite bank of the Seine. The Louvre's new eastern wing was scarcely begun when Colbert, the new superintendent of buildings, who harboured unfriendly feelings towards Le Vau, ordered the suspension of his project. He called for new proposals whose magnificence would be worthy of the palace's official entrance, to be located in the eastern wing. Several architects submitted projects to Colbert's competition, including the Frenchmen Mansard and Marot and the Italians Pietro da Cortona and Bernini. After numerous hesitations, Colbert appointed Le Brun, Le Vau, and Perrault to a committee, which accepted the new plans. After 1668, the project would be directed by Perrault alone, since by then Le Vau was working on the new palace site at Versailles. In the meantime, work on the courtyard façade of the eastern wing continued according to the earlier plans of Lescot and Le Mercier, but it was not completed until 1757. On the outer side, Perrault's colonnade, justly regarded as one of the summits of architecture under Louis XIV, was built. To harmonise with the colonnade, a new façade was added to the southern wing, which covered the earlier one built by Lescot and Le Vau. The changes to the Louvre throughout this period were the fruit of Colbert's political determination, rather than Louis XIV's express wishes. The king showed little interest in his Parisian palace, and in 1678 its reconstruction was once again interrupted. Four years later, Louis XIV officially moved to Versailles.

From the invasion of the Louvre to the Muséum Central des Arts

With the court now at Versailles, the beginning of the 18th century saw what Louis Hautecœur has called 'the invasion of the Louvre'. Numerous organisations began taking over the building, including the Academy of Sciences and the Academy of Painting and Sculpture, which regularly held Salons within its walls. Many artists had ateliers in the Louvre, including the sculptors Pigalle and Falconet and the painter François Boucher. The apartments were used as private residences. This state of affairs resulted in the neglect of the buildings and raised numerous protests. Late in the 1750's, Soufflot was commissioned to complete the northern wing and the courtyard side of the eastern wing. At the same time, numerous residential buildings, considered detrimental to the aesthetic harmony of the colonnade, were demolished. Yet no one seemed to know what to do with the buildings of the Louvre, in which the monarchs no longer wished to reside. In 1774, Comte d'Angiviller was appointed Superintendent of the King's Buildings. He would be responsible for the realisation of an idea that had been envisaged for a number of years: the public display of the

Map by Turgot

1737-1739

(detail)

The construction of the Palais des Tuileries has now been completed, but the residential buildings between the Louvre and the Tuileries, which will be demolished in the 19th century, are still standing. The surface area of the Louvre's Cour Carré has quadrupled. Unfinished roofing is visible on the Saint-Honoré and Saint Germain l'Auxerrois sides.

best paintings in the royal collections. In 1776, the scale models exhibited in the Grande Galerie were moved to the Invalides, and in 1779 the refurbishing of the gallery was entrusted to a committee, which included Soufflot, the sculptor Pajou, and the painter Hubert Robert. In spite of D'Angiviller's solid policy for the acquisition of paintings, work on the new museum was slow in getting started–and was, of course, interrupted by the French Revolution. The new government adopted D'Angiviller's project, however, and, on 16 September 1792, the Musée du Louvre was founded. Its opening to the public on 10 August 1793 coincided with the Salon, whose function was to exhibit living artists.

The 'Grand Design' resuscitated

Following the upheaval of the revolutionary period, the idea of connecting the Louvre to the Tuileries, part of the 'Grand Design', was revived by the successive new governments. Napoleon I entrusted the architects Percier and Fontaine, the main upholders of Empire style, with the still-unfinished site. In the Cour Carrée, they completed the roofing of both the northern and western wings, as well as the carvings on the courtyard side and on the main façades. After evicting the Louvre's remaining lodgers, they began reorganising the space and redecorating the rooms and apartments to house the works of art that were beginning to pour in from all over Europe. Percier and Fontaine also proceeded to oust the numerous merchants who had set up shop in the covered passageways of the Louvre. Finally, they decided to demolish the residential buildings in the Cour du Carrousel. In 1806, they erected a triumphal arch and began the construction, on the Rue de Rivoli side, of a gallery linking the Pavillon de Marsan, at the northern end of the Tuileries Gardens, with the Pavillon de Rohan, where one of the gateways to the Louvre is located. Completed in 1825, the gallery's courtyard side was stylistically influenced by the Grande Galerie facing it, which was built by Androuet Du Cerceau. A stricter style was adopted for the Rue de Rivoli façade.

During the Restoration and the July Monarchy, a large number of works of art that had been confiscated by the Napoleonic armies were restored to their owners. Little major construction work took place during this time, except for the completion of Percier and Fontaine's northern wing and the installation of the Naval Museum on the second floor of the Louvre. The main task at hand was the refurbishment and decoration of the exhibition rooms. Under the direction of Champollion the Egyptian collections were arranged in a lavish gallery named after Charles X: decorated in gold and marble, its arches and ceilings embellished with allegorical scenes painted by artists such as Abel de Pujol and Vinchon, the gallery is characteristic of the eclectic taste of a society in search of diversity after the sobriety of the Empire style.

Two hundred and fifty years after he had first conceived it, Henri IV's 'Grand Design' was finally completed by Napoleon III. It was, however, to be short-lived.

A new phase of refurbishing began with the decoration of several exhibition rooms, including the Galerie d'Apollon, whose central ceiling, completed in 1851, was painted by Delacroix –already renowned for the frescoes in the Palais Bourbon and the Chamber of Peers. In 1852, Louis Visconti was commissioned to finish closing the square formed by the Louvre and the Tuileries; he was succeeded the following year by Hector Lefuel. This ambitious, well-thought-out project was finally completed five years later, at the time when Haussman's ambitious urban plans were revamping the rest of Paris.

The residential buildings still standing between the Arc du Carrousel and the Louvre were now razed. In order to 'correct' certain optical distortions created by perspective, two new wings were built in the Cour Napoleon: the southern wing, known as Denon, was connected to the Grande Galerie by cross buildings; the northern wing, following the same plan, was named Richelieu. Each wing had three pavilions and several interior courtyards, as well as arcades on the ground floor that were extended along the earlier façade built by Lescot and Le Mercier. The whole was then exuberantly decorated with a profusion of carvings; statues of great men were later added to the terraces above the arcades. The interior of the new buildings was equally exuberant and profusely decorated: paintings, sculptures, stucco decorations, and gold embellishments flaunted the wealth of the Second Empire. But Hector Lefuel's work was not yet done. In 1861, despite strong criticism, he undertook the complete reconstruction of the Pavillon de Flore and the section of the Grande Galerie built by Du Cerceau. Next to the Grande Galerie, opposite the Arc du Carrousel, he built the Nouvelle Salle des États and, farther west, facing the Seine, between the two pavilions known as La Trémoille and Lesdiguières, a three-arched gateway.

The link between the Louvre and the Tuileries palace had scarcely been completed when the Commune erupted in 1871. Despite the insurgents' efforts to protect the Louvre, on 23 May, during the suppression of the Commune in its final days, a number of buildings were set on fire and the Tuileries palace burned to the ground. The government that succeeded the Second Empire called upon Lefuel to restore the galleries and pavilions, but the Third Republic decided that it would be too costly to rebuild the Tuileries palace, felt to be too closely associated with the monarchy. The area in front of the Louvre was thus left wide open to face the Place de la Concorde and beyond.

The Grand Louvre becomes a reality

From the Third Republic to the 1970's, all changes undertaken at the Louvre concerned aspects of internal disposition or the rearrangement of collections. It was not until the election of President François Mitterrand in 1981 that the Louvre became once again an affair of State.

The new project, known as the Grand Louvre, aimed to create a space dedicated entirely to the arts, with larger exhibition areas and rearranged collections. This was made possible by the rationalisation of the available space and the acquisition of the ministerial offices that had been occupied by the government since the days of Napoleon III. Another aim of the Grand Louvre project was to improve the museum's relations with the public and, especially, the reception of visitors.

In 1983, the architect Ieoh Ming Pei was entrusted with the vast enterprise; the first phase included the renovation of the Cour Napoleon and the construction in the courtyard of the now-famous glass pyramid, whose proportions are identical to those of the Pyramid of Giza in Egypt. The reorganisation of the exhibition rooms was begun at the same time, as was the construction of the vast shopping area under the Cour du Carrousel. Meanwhile, on the surface, landscape architects proceeded with the renovation of the Tuileries Gardens, extending from the Louvre to the Place de la Concorde.

When the Grand Louvre was inaugurated in 1993, on the occasion of the celebration of the second centenary of the Muséum Central des Arts, its total exhibition area had been increased from 30,000 to 60,000 square metres (35,880 to 71,760 square yards). Tens of thousands of works are now on display for the five million visitors who flock to the museum every year. The underground shopping area covers an area as large as the museum building itself. The originality of the Grand Louvre project lies above all in its ambition to create a coherent architectural and aesthetic whole out of what was a relatively disparate aggregate despite the ingenious efforts of generations of architects, each of whom attempted to continue the work of his predecessors while leaving the imprint of his own time. The Cour Carrée provides a good illustration: the four small walls begun under François I in the 16th century were not completed until the 19th century under Napoleon I.

13

The Louvre from Philippe Auguste to Charles VII

THE LIMBOURG BROTHERS

The Very Rich Hours of the Duc de Berry

1413-1416
Musée Condé, Chantilly.

A calendar page from an illuminated manuscript depicting the early fifteenth-century Louvre, as seen from the Hôtel de Nesle (the residence of Charles V's brother, the Duc de Berry) on the opposite bank of the Seine. At the time, the Louvre was a castle protected by ramparts enclosing the city of Paris; it was inhabited by Isabeau of Bavaria, wife of Charles VI the Well-Beloved. The building shown here has the form defined by Charles V fifty years previously: the towers of Philippe Auguste's earlier fortress have been raised and decorated, and windows pierced to let light into the apartments.

The Louvre has now become a royal residence, as the illustration shows.

The Grosse Tour (Big Tower), symbolising the protective role of the monarchy, points its pennant skyward in the direction of the sun, from which its power seems to emanate. The river symbolically divides the painting into two sections, with the foreground representing terrestrial activities: the peasant's harrow mirrors the quadrangular shape of the castle, and a rock sits in its centre, just as the Grosse Tour in the middle of the castle towers over it. The position and shape of the seed bag on the ground seem to correspond to the sun, with both seed bag and sun providing nourishment for the kingdom.

ANONYMOUS, FLEMISH SCHOOL

Retable of the Parliament of Paris

Mid-15th century, Musée du Louvre (detail)

When the *Retable* was commissioned in 1453, during the reign of Charles VII, the Louvre was no longer a royal residence; it had become an arsenal and a prison. It is depicted here in a less idealised manner than in the preceding work: no attempt has been made to lighten the massive aspect of the fortress. In *The Very Rich Hours*, the Tour du Coin (Corner Tower), which joined up with the ramparts, was on the right-hand side; here, it is on the left, leaving a clear view of the eastern part of the castle. The outline of the Grosse Tour is visible in the background. To the right of the Louvre, the artist has depicted the Hôtel du Petit-Bourbon, a mansion constructed in 1303 by Louis I, Duke of Bourbon, and rebuilt in 1390. After changing owners many times, it was partially torn down in the 16th century. Some buildings remained and were put to other uses: one becoming a theatre where Molière's *Précieuses ridicules* was first performed in 1659. Most of the remaining vestiges of the Petit-Bourbon were torn down in 1661, when Le Vau extended the southern wing of the Louvre.

The Louvre from François I to Louis XIII

ANONYMOUS,
FLEMISH
SCHOOL

**The Pont Neuf and
the Louvre**

Circa 1635, Paris,
Musée Carnavalet (detail)

Beginning with the reign
of François I, the Louvre
was to undergo a series
of radical transformations,
as can be seen here.
The painting depicts the
Louvre from roughly the
same angle as does
The Very Rich Hours,
showing the façade
overlooking the Seine and
the eastern side. From this
angle, all that remains from
the earlier time is the
medieval tower, next to
which stand Pierre Lescot's
building and the Pavillon
du Roi beyond. They have
replaced the southern wall
of the fortress. At the foot
of the tower, the Hôtel du
Petit-Bourbon is still
standing; beyond is a series
of buildings and another
tower dating from
Charles V's reign.
Charles IX's Petite Galerie
forms a right angle with
the Pavillon du Roi.
Behind, in a straight line
running from the Pavillon
du Roi, one can just make
out the roof of the Pavillon
de l'Horloge –recently
erected by Louis XIII–
at the far end of Lescot's
western wing. Also visible
in the background, to the
left, are the Tuileries
Gardens and the Pavillon
de Flore, constituting
the far end of Catherine
de' Medici's palace.
The Pavillon de Flore has
been linked to the Petite
Galerie by the riverside
gallery, now know as the
Grande Galerie. Next to
the Pont Neuf, on the right,
the top part of the
Samaritaine's first water
pump can be seen.

Salle des Caryatides

Lescot's first construction, built on the site of the western wall of the medieval castle, contained a ground-floor hall with a raised platform supported by four caryatids sculpted by Jean Goujon in 1550. During the reign of Louis XIII, Le Mercier replaced the wooden ceiling with a stone vault. During the Empire, the architects Percier and Fontaine completed the decor, placed Benvenuto Cellini's *Diane d'Anet* above the raised platform, and constructed the little Salle du Tribunal on the same level. The Institut de France, which had been housed here since 1796, moved out of the Salle de Caryatides in 1806 to allow for the exhibition of antiques.

Decoration of Anne of Austria's summer apartment

In 1655, Le Vau began decorating the summer apartment of the queen mother, situated on the ground floor of the Petite Galerie. The ceiling was entrusted to Giovanni Francesco Romanelli, who had just finished painting the ceiling of the Galerie Mazarine (today, the Bibliothèque Nationale de France). Romanelli also provided the drawings from which Michel Anguier executed the stucco decorations.

Pavillon de l'Horloge, known as Pavillon de Sully

The construction of the Pavillon de Sully began in 1624. It stands in the centre of the Lescot-Le Mercier wing on the western flank of the Cour Carré. Here, Le Mercier has deliberately taken his inspiration from Pierre Lescot, while giving a more personal touch to the upper levels with the three large bay windows decorated with caryatids –executed by Jacques Sarrazin and his students– and the unusual pediment with two sculpted allegorical figures representing Fame. During the Second Empire, the architect Henri Lefuel had the square-based dome adorned with lead ornamentation.
The architectural design of Le Mercier's pavilion would strongly influence architects who later worked on the Louvre, from Le Mercier's contemporary Le Vau to Napoleon III's architects. To a certain extent, it may be said that the Louvre is the conjunction of both Lescot and Le Mercier's concepts.

Louis XIV's Louvre

**REINIER
NOOMS
KNOWN AS
ZEEMAN**

View of the Louvre

Circa 1666
Musée du Château
de Versailles (detail).

Since the reign of
Louis XIII, nothing has
changed between the
Tuileries Gardens and the
far end of the Grande
Galerie. The Petite Galerie
has doubled in width,
however, and a new
pavilion (the Pavillon des
Arts) has been added by
Le Vau next to Lescot's
building, which has been
extended eastward,
towards the site of the
Petit-Bourbon.
The Lescot-Le Vau wing as
depicted here is in a state
of transition. It will be
given a new façade in 1668
when Claude Perrault's
colonnade is erected on its
eastern flank. On the
banks of the Seine closest
to the Petite Galerie, a wall
can be seen running
parallel to Lescot's
building; it is the façade of
an orangery built by
Marie de' Medici in 1617
on the foundations of
Charles V's earlier
ramparts –the section that
is visible in *The Very Rich
Hours* of the Duc de Berry,
ending at the Tour de
Coin (Corner Tower).

PIERRE-ANTOINE DE MACHY

View of the Colonnade of the Louvre

1772 / Paris, Musée de Louvre.

In December 1758, an order was given to clear the access to the colonnade,
but work on the site did not begin until 1760; it was completed in 1773.
In this painting, the roof of a corner pavilion of the colonnade is being dismantled.
When the colonnade was built in 1668, a new façade was added on the Seine side,
covering the one that Le Vau had just completed.
In 1678, when Louis XIV moved to Versailles, all construction work came to a halt, and Le Vau's roofing remained
untouched. The ornamentation of the southern and eastern wings was not completed until the Empire, then partially
modified during the Restoration (particularly the pediment of the colonnade's central pavilion).

HUBERT ROBERT

The Grande Galerie at the Louvre

Circa 1795 / Paris, Musée du Louvre.

Hubert Robert, the curator of paintings of the Muséum Royal from 1784 to 1792, was imprisoned at Sainte Pélagie
from 1793 to 1794. Later, between 1795 and 1802, he served on the committee of the Conservatory and directed
the Muséum Central des Arts. Several years before the French Revolution, he had made a study of lighting problems
in the Grande Galerie, but in his subsequent paintings, the initial object of study was obscured
by his taste for romantic ruins. Although the Muséum opened in 1793, it was only in 1799
that a permanent exhibition was displayed in the Grande Galerie.

24

AUGUSTE COUDER

Napoleon Visiting the Staircase of the Louvre

1833 / Musée National du Château de Malmaison

In 1803, the Muséum Central des Arts was renamed the Musée Napoleon. Three years later, Percier and Fontaine built the Arc du Carrousel and began the construction of a northern gallery that would link the Louvre and the Tuileries palace. In the scene depicted here, the architects stand in front of the new staircase (near today's Pavillon Daru) that they had just completed in 1812. They are shown presenting their work to the Emperor; behind him are the Comte Daru and the museum director, Vivant Denon. The staircase was later torn down during the Second Empire. The work undertaken at the Louvre under Napoleon I was part of a major urban project that would have included the construction of a palace on the hill at Chaillot for Napoleon's son, known in his childhood as the King of Rome.

VICTOR-JOSEPH CHAVET

Napoleon III's Louvre

1857 / Paris, Musée du Louvre

The architect Visconti, one of Percier's students, came to Napoleon's attention while working on the Emperor's tomb
at the Invalides. In 1852, he was commissioned to complete a centuries-old project, the Louvre-Tuileries link.
The first stone was laid on 25 July 1852, but in December of the following year Visconti died, and the difficult task of
directing the site, still in its early stages, fell to Hector Lefuel.
The new Louvre was inaugurated by Napoleon III on 14 August 1857. Chavet's painting, executed in the same year,
offers a panoramic view of the buildings from the Tuileries Gardens to the Cour Carrée.

The Grand Louvre

The Pyramid and the Pavillon Richelieu, in the Cour Napoleon

The decision to create a new 'Grand' Louvre was made in 1981. The project was marked by a series of major stages, the most spectacular being the construction of Ieoh Ming Pei's pyramid, a monumental glass-and-steel structure surrounded by the elegantly sculpted façades of the Cour Napoleon. Another major step was the departure of the Ministry of Finance from the Cour Richelieu, which increased the museum's exhibition area by 22,000 square metres (26,300 square yards).

Pierre Lescot's façade in the Cour Carrée

Before construction work on the Grand Louvre could begin, the site was turned into a vast archaeological dig covering nearly three hectares (over seven acres). Philippe Auguste's fortress covered a square-shaped area whose western and southern walls corresponded to the two wings built by Lescot around 1550. Both the Cour Carrée and the Cour Napoleon had to be thoroughly excavated to uncover the structure of the medieval castle and its surroundings. While the archaeologists were excavating the courtyards, the façades of the Louvre were being cleaned and the damaged carvings and statues restored.

View of the Cour Marly, in the Richelieu wing

The Richelieu wing, bordering the Rue de Rivoli, is made up of three glassed-in courtyards surrounded by Hector Lefuel's façades. The Cour Marly and the Cour Puget display French sculpture from the 17th to the 19th centuries, while the Cour Khorsabad houses the Assyrian winged bulls from Sargon II's palace. The Cour Marly, covering an area of 2,200 square metres (2,630 square yards), is the largest of the courtyards. Conceived by architect Michel Macary, it was designed to display several monumental sculpted groups, including four river allegories and two marble groups of winged horses by Antoine Coysevox, as well as two famous equine groups by Guillaume Coustou, better known as the *Chevaux de Marly* (the horses of Marly), which used to stand at the entrance to the Champs-Elysées.

**The Cour Napoleon
with the Pavillon
Turgot and the
Pavillon Richelieu**

In the background,
scaffolding covers the
Pavillon Colbert,
undergoing restoration at
the time. In Visconti's
original design, the arcades
were to have contained
statues of famous men,
'following the example of
the forums of Antiquity'.
But when Lefuel took over
the project, he decided to
place the statues on the
terraced area on top of the
arcades. Over the years,
many of the eighty-four
statues of French historical
figures had been seriously
damaged; some, including
those of Rabelais and
Poussin, had been
completely destroyed.
It took five teams of
restorers and ten sculptors
working on the Grand
Louvre project to
rehabilitate the statues.

The Cour du Sphinx

The beautifully restored
Courtyard of the Sphinx,
now housing Greek and
Roman antiquities, had
been closed since the
Second Empire, when it
was known as the Queen's
Courtyard. Shown here is
the western façade of the
Petite Galerie, whose width
was doubled by Le Vau
in the 17th century.
The pediment, carved by
Lespagnandelle in 1663,
shows the sun flanked by
the attributes of the arts
and sciences. *The Mosaic of
the Seasons,* which once
embellished a Roman villa,
covers the central area
of the courtyard.

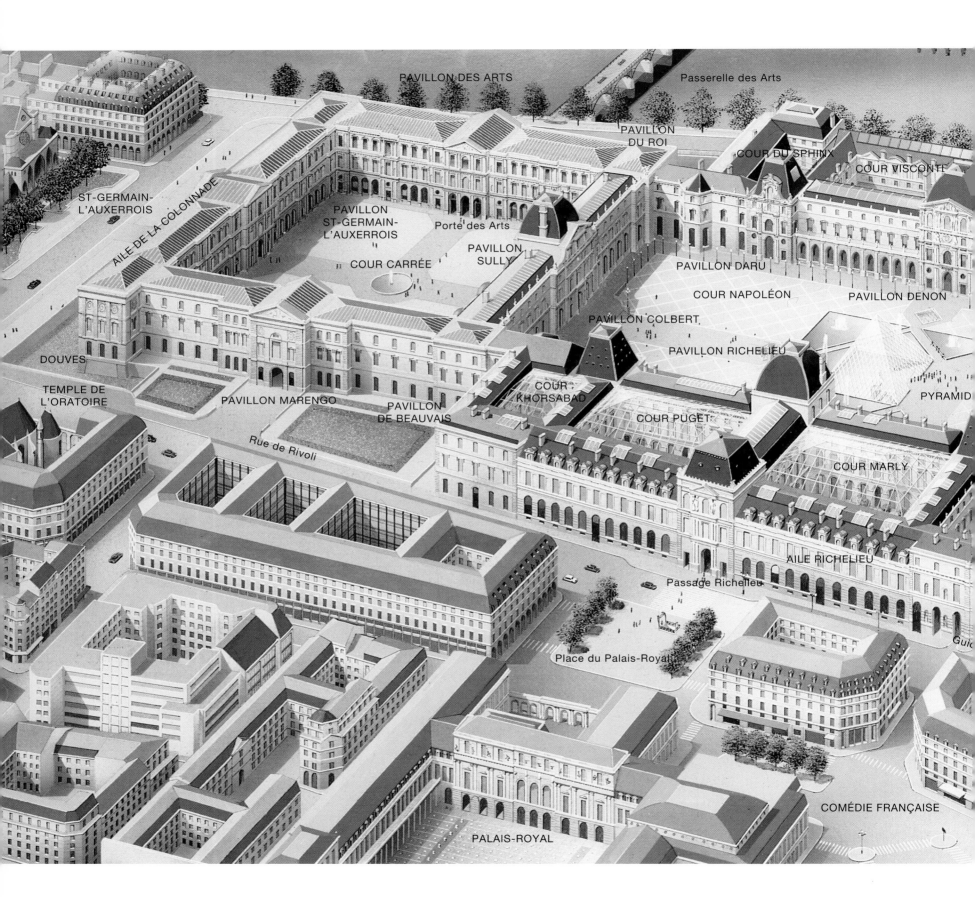

PAVILLON DES ARTS
Passerelle des Arts
PAVILLON DU ROI
COUR DU SPHINX
COUR VISCONTI
ST-GERMAIN-L'AUXERROIS
AILE DE LA COLONNADE
PAVILLON ST-GERMAIN-L'AUXERROIS
Porte des Arts
PAVILLON SULLY
COUR CARRÉE
PAVILLON DARU
COUR NAPOLÉON
PAVILLON DENON
PAVILLON COLBERT
DOUVES
PAVILLON RICHELIEU
TEMPLE DE L'ORATOIRE
PAVILLON MARENGO
PAVILLON DE BEAUVAIS
COUR KHORSABAD
PYRAMID
COUR PUGET
Rue de Rivoli
COUR MARLY
AILE RICHELIEU
Passage Richelieu
Guic
Place du Palais-Royal
COMÉDIE FRANÇAISE
PALAIS-ROYAL

Pont du Carrousel

PAVILLON LESDIGUIÈRES

COUR LEFUEL

PAVILLON LA TRÉMOILLE

LA SEINE

Pont Royal

PAVILLON DE FLORE

Guichets du Carrousel

PAVILLON MOLLIEN

NOUVELLE
SALLE
DES ÉTATS

Porte Jaujard

Accès parc de
stationnement
en sous-sol

VILLON TURGOT

ROND-POINT

PYRAMIDE INVERSÉE

ESPLANADE
DU
CARROUSEL

ARC DE TRIOMPHE
DU CARROUSEL

rny

VILLON DE ROHAN

JARDINS DU CARROUSEL

LA TERRASSE

Avenue du Général-Lemonnier

MUSÉE DES ARTS DÉCORATIFS

JARDINS
DES
TUILERIES

PAVILLON DE MARSAN

Rue de Rivoli

Map of Grand Louvre

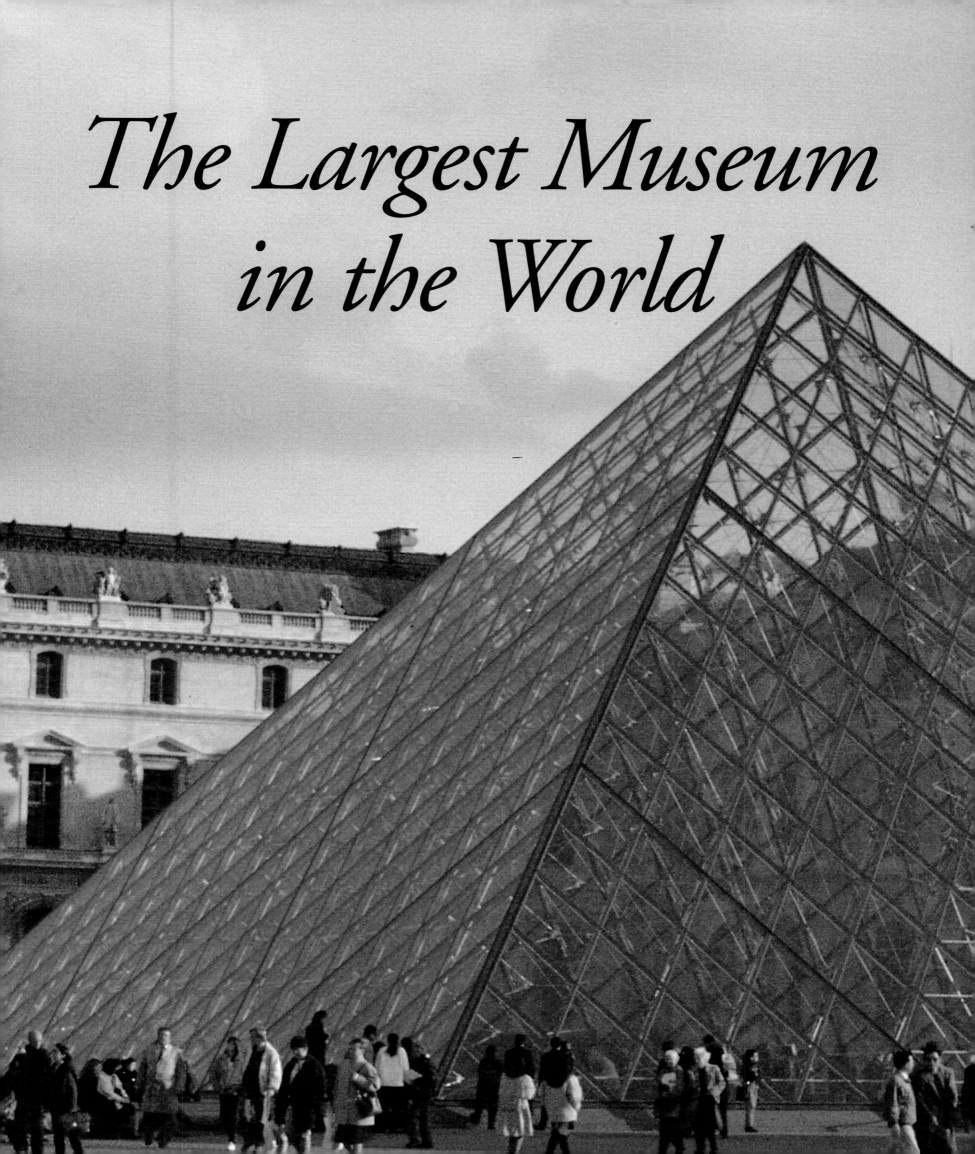

The Largest Museum
in the World

The concept of an art collection dates from the 14th century and can be attributed to art lovers like King John the Good, who was known as an ardent collector. His son Charles V had a library at the Louvre of about 1,000 manuscripts. Of his collection of works of art nothing remains but a list of entries; however, judging from the descriptions that have come down to us, he owned many magnificent objects. The 14th century was a time of intense intellectual and artistic activity in France, and the king's brothers, Philippe of Burgundy and Louis of Anjou –both of whom commissioned illuminated manuscripts from the Limbourg brothers– were also reputed collectors.

These early collections had little internal organisation, however; they were merely accumulations of precious objects, regarded as curiosities to be displayed in collectors' cabinets. The modern meaning of the word 'collection' –implying the classifying of objects and the completion of individual subdivisions– does not appear in Europe until the Renaissance in the 16th century, when the desire to categorise knowledge came to the forefront.

DENIS
FOULLECHAT

Charles V in his library at the Louvre, in the Tour de la Fauconnerie (the north-west corner tower of the medieval château)

1372 / Bibliothèque Nationale de France.

Illuminated manuscript of a French translation of John of Salisbury's *Policraticus*.

Preceding pages

The Cour Napoleon: I.M. Pei's pyramid and the Pavillon de Sully, built by Le Mercier.

The origins of the royal collections

Charles VIII's Italian campaign in 1494 played a major role in the development of the French Renaissance. His successor, Louis XII, who continued the wars in Italy, was responsible for beginning the royal collections. It is thanks to him that the Louvre today possesses several works by Fra Bartolomeo and Leonardo da Vinci.

Louis XII's son-in-law and successor, François I, initiated a true programme of acquisitions. A generous art patron who wished to emulate the Italian princes of his age, François I assembled a significant collection of gold and silverware, medals, stone carvings, Greek and Roman sculpture, and casts, which he housed for the most part at his château in Fontainebleau. This collection would constitute the beginnings of the Louvre's Department of Antiquities. Contemporary sculpture was well represented in François I's collection: Benvenuto Cellini worked for a time at the French court, and two major additions to the collection,

Michelangelo's *Bound Slave* and *Dying Slave,* reached France shortly after the king's death. Italian artists dominated François I's collection of paintings, which included frescoes executed for the Château of Fontainebleau by Rosso Fiorentino and Francesco Primaticcio, and two of the Louvre's most celebrated works, commissioned by Pope Leo X for the French king, *Saint Michael Victorious* and *The Great Holy Family of François I,* both by Raphael, whose work François I greatly admired–and whom he tried unsuccessfully to entice to France. The collection also contained numerous masterpieces by Leonardo da Vinci, who died near Amboise (in the king's arms, if the legend can be believed), including the world-famous portrait of Lisa Gherardini, known as *Mona Lisa* or *La Gioconda.* Works by many other artists were included in the collection; unfortunately, a number of paintings by Correggio, Michelangelo, and Perugino were lost over the centuries.

The king's collection was regularly enriched with gifts from foreign diplomats and works directly commissioned from artists. In some cases, new acquisitions were made through intermediaries and merchants such as Giovanni Battista della Palla or Aretino –whom Ariosto referred to as the 'scourge of princes'.

When François I died in 1547, his collection was continued by his son Henri II, who invited Nicollò Dell' Abate to assist Primaticcio, but the volume of acquisitions was henceforth curbed. In addition to commissioning works for the royal residences, Henri IV also wished to constitute a collection of antiques, but his early death meant that the project never materialised. The situation was much the same under Louis XIII, who was nonetheless an art lover –he even took drawing lessons from Simon Vouet and commissioned Poussin to decorate the Grande Galerie at the Louvre. Although Richelieu and the king succeeded in injecting a sense of vigour into the arts in France in response to Italy's dominance, they were too deeply preoccupied with politics and affairs of state to give the arts much attention.

A major programme of patronage

François I's ambitions were finally fulfilled by Louis XIV. The task of defining a policy of patronage was left to Colbert, who was named Financial Administrator in 1661 and Superintendent of Buildings in 1664. He was succeeded by Louvois, who continued his work.

The Crown's collections were first enriched in 1660 with the inheritance of coins and medals belonging to Gaston d'Orléans. Later, Mazarin –a great collector of antiques and Chinese objects who has often been unjustly accused of being an art hoarder rather than an art lover– transferred many works from his own collection to the king's, including statues from Antiquity, paintings, and tapestries. In 1665, the Duc de Richelieu, a great-nephew of the Cardinal, was obliged to cede his paintings after losing a bet with Louis XIV over a game of royal tennis (the ancestor of modern tennis). The Crown thus acquired thirteen paintings by Poussin, including the series of canvasses depicting the four seasons, which are among the painter's masterpieces. The growth of the collections was rapid. In 1671, Jabach, a banker, made a sale consisting of '101 paintings and 5,542 drawings by the great masters'.

The acquisitions policy was backed up by diplomatic missions in Europe and the Near East. Some works entered the royal collection individually, but many more were acquired in blocks. Entire collections were sometimes transferred to the Crown, including the Abbot de Marolles' collection of 123,400 engravings in 1667, and drawings from Le Brun's atelier in 1690 and from Mignard's in 1693. When the king's landscape architect, Le Nôtre, gave him his paintings in 1693, Louis XIV declared himself to be 'delighted by so magnificent a present'. The king's collection was characterised by its wide-ranging variety; when it was transferred to Versailles in 1681, it consisted of more than 20,000 medals, stone carvings, vellums, antiques, statues, and busts. When Colbert took office, the royal collection contained 200 paintings. By the time Louis XIV died in 1715, it had grown tenfold. The Northern School was represented by Holbein, Brueghel, Van Dyck, and Rembrandt, among others. The French School included Poussin and Le Lorrain, while the Italian School was represented by Leonardo da Vinci, Titian, Veronese, Caravaggio, and many others.

The end of the Ancien Régime

Louis XIV's initial enthusiasm was succeeded by less resolute ambitions on the part of others. Fashionable artists such as Nattier, Boucher, and Van Loo continued to receive commissions to decorate the royal residences. Several acquisitions were made during this period: in 1742, for example, through the mediation of the painter Rigaud, a number of works were acquired from Louis de Carignan's collection before it was dispersed the following year. Some paintings from his collection are still at the Louvre, including Raphael's *Virgin with the Veil* and Rubens' *Flight of Lot*. When works belonging to the renowned collector Pierre-Jean Mariette were sold in 1775, the Crown acquired about 1,000 drawings by the greatest European masters.

Changing attitudes around the middle of the 18th century were to have important repercussions for the royal collections. One of the earliest signs of the changes to come was the publication of *Reflections on Some of the Causes of the Present State of Painting in France, and on the Fine Arts* by La Font de Saint-Yenne. The author expresses his desire to bring together the masterpieces 'that make up His Majesty's Cabinet' in a single place so as to make them accessible to all art lovers. Numerous such projects mentioned the Louvre as a possible venue, not only for reasons of prestige, but also because the buildings were in so advanced a state of dis-

repair that the idea of demolishing them had arisen several times. In 1750, an exhibition of 110 French, Italian, and Flemish paintings was held at the Luxembourg Palace, where Rubens' series on the life of Marie de' Medici was already on display. Regarded as France's first museum, the Luxembourg Palace remained open to the public until 1779. Though the experience was short-lived, it served to point up a new need, to which the Comte d'Angiviller would try to respond in 1774 when Louis XVI acceded to the throne and appointed him Superintendent of the King's Buildings. D'Angiviller hoped to display the Crown's paintings and sculptures in a newly created museum installed at the Louvre, now 'abandoned and become the refuge of owls', according to La Font de Saint-Yenne.

Although the renovation of the buildings was long and slow, D'Angiviller did not hesitate to acquire new works for the royal collections.

He was responsible for the already-mentioned Mariette collection; he enriched the Spanish collections with three paintings by Murillo, and the French collections with twenty-two works in the Saint Bruno cycle by Le Sueur. To restore the balance among the different schools, D'Angiviller favoured painters from Northern Europe, who had been poorly represented until then, especially in comparison with the dominant Italian school.

He was responsible for acquiring Rubens' *Helena Fourment and her Children;* several works by Rembrandt, including *The Pilgrims at Emmaus;* and paintings by Jordaens, Metsu, David Teniers, and Ruysdael.

The Salon of 1699 in the Grande Galerie

Engraving from an almanac published in Paris in 1700.

After being forsaken by the king, the Louvre served to house several institutions, including the Academy of Painting and Sculpture, which moved in in 1692 and held Salons exhibiting the works of its members, notably in 1699 and 1704.

The Comte
d'Angiviller
(1720-1809),
Superintendent of
the King's Buildings

Painting by
Joseph Sigfred Duplessis.
Musée du Louvre.

From the French Revolution to the July Monarchy

In 1791, the National Assembly adopted D'Angiviller's project and decreed the creation of the Muséum Central, dedicated to 'the reunion of all scientific and artistic monuments'. In 1793, the Louvre was opened to the public for the first time. But a number of problems arose relating to the organisation of the museum and the administration of the new institution. Although it was stated that museums were places where the 'imagination rises in conjunction with the sensations experienced', according to the contemporary writer Alexandre Lenoir, they were required, above all, to fulfil an educational role.

The French Revolution was a boon for the collections of the new museum. Property belonging to the clergy and emigrants was seized, and works of art and furniture from the royal residences were requisitioned. It was all housed in

Italian masterpieces arriving at the Louvre

Detail of a painting by Swebach-Desfontaine. Musée du Louvre.

the Convent of the Petits-Augustins (today, the École des Beaux-Arts), directed by Alexandre Lenoir, before being transferred to the museum. After some hesitation, the collections from the Palace of Versailles and the two Trianons were transferred to Paris in July 1794.

Numerous 'diplomatic seizures' throughout Europe, then in the grips of war, were added to the national collections. In August 1794, Abbot Grégoire wrote: 'Through bravery, the Republic acquires what Louis XIV, despite great riches, could never obtain. Crayer, Van Dyck and Rubens are all on the road to Paris.' He adds: 'If our victorious armies were to enter Italy, the removal of *Apollo Belvedere* and *Hercules Farnese* would be our greatest conquest.'

The collections grew significantly in the years of upheaval between the National Convention and the Empire. Among the many works acquired during this period were Fra Angelico's *Coronation of the Virgin,* Veronese's *Marriage at Cana,* and Prince Borghese's collection of antiques. The acquisition of art works by the Louvre closely followed Napoleon's victories and military campaigns in Belgium, Italy, Egypt, Germany, Austria, and Spain. At the museum, works were rearranged and new rooms such as the Salon Carré and the Galerie d'Apollon opened to the public. In 1803, the Louvre became the Musée Napoleon. This era came to an end in 1815 with Napoleon's defeat at Waterloo. The vanquished Empire was dismantled, and the victorious European powers demanded the restitution of their property. Despite resistance, notably from the museum's director, Vivant Denon, the Bourbon Restoration tried –at least sporadically– to comply with these demands, while at the same time encouraging new acquisitions. Louis XVIII inaugurated a period of art patronage–in a few years the Louvre acquired more than one hundred paintings–and it was during his reign, in 1821, that the majestically sensuous *Venus de Milo* entered the museum.

When he acceded to the throne, Charles X continued his brother's policy of acquisitions–albeit more modestly; he also had the collections reorganised and rearranged. In 1824, *The Raft of the Medusa* by Théodore Géricault was purchased at a posthumous sale of the artist's works. This was a controversial acquisition, as the shipwreck of the frigate *Medusa* was thought to symbolise the nation's downfall. The following year, the Department of Egyptian Antiquities was inaugurated under Champollion's direction. Beginning in 1830, under the July Monarchy, the government's efforts were increasingly directed towards the restoration of the palace at Versailles, where it planned to install a historical museum dedicated to patriotic displays. But the Louvre was not forgotten, and in 1847, following the discovery at Khorsabad of the ruins of Sargon II's palace, a new Assyrian section was opened. From then on, the Louvre was closely associated with the developing interest in Middle Eastern and Oriental studies and with the key role that would be played by French archaeology. The museum's collections were thereafter enriched by finds from numerous excavations, as well as by private donations.

Prestigious acquisitions

Under the Second Empire, the nation experienced a period of great economic prosperity, to the benefit of the Louvre. The Louvre-Tuileries link was finally completed, and the rooms in the various departments were restored.

According to Philippe de Chennevières, director of the École des Beaux-Arts, between 1850 and 1863 the museum was enriched by 20,000 works of art. The inventory of the collections, donations, and purchases is long, but the quality of the works listed is impressive. In 1861, the private museum of the Marquis Campana, which the French government had just acquired, arrived in Paris. The collection, famed for its Greek, Roman, and Etruscan antiquities (it included the *Sarcophagus of a Married Couple),* contained several thousand items: bronzes, painted vases, hundreds of pieces of antique jewellery, and 14th- and 15th-century Italian majolicas and paintings, including Uccello's *Battle of San Romano.*

Between 1853 and 1868, in the field of painting alone, the number of acquisitions totalled 688, while donations rose to 82; they included *The Carcass of Beef* by Rembrandt and *The Harpsichord Lesson* by Fragonard.

In 1869, Doctor Louis La Caze died, leaving a collection of 272 French, Spanish, Flemish, and Dutch paintings. Among the many masterpieces were Watteau's *Pierrot* and Rembrandt's *Bathsheba at her Bath.*

From the Third Republic to the present

Under the Second Empire, the Louvre's administrators had followed a strong-minded line fashioned after Colbert's. The policy of the Third Republic was to encourage private donations and bequests. A complete list would take up too many pages, but the following examples of donations should provide an eloquent testimonial: His de la Salle's renowned collection of drawings entered the Louvre in 1878; Coutan's collection –which included several works by Géricault and Prud'hon– in 1883; Baron Davillier's in 1885; and Madame Boucicaut's in 1889. Some major works, such as the *Pietà of Villeneuve-lès-Avignon,* presented by the Société des Amis du Louvre in 1905, did not enter the museum as part of a collection, but as a separate donation.

The Department of Painting was not the only one to benefit from donations. The Departments of Greek, Roman, Egyptian, and Oriental Antiquities were greatly enriched by archaeological finds. *The Winged Victory of Samothrace* was discovered in 1863 on an island in the Aegean Sea by an expedition led by Noël Champoiseau. Edmond de Rothschild, in addition to presenting the museum with his excellent collection of drawings, sponsored archaeological expeditions. In 1912, Baroness Alphonse Delort de Gléon presented the museum with a collection of Islamic art works. Over the centuries, many collectors and archaeologists have worked to preserve the world's cultural heritage.

This euphoric period of donations and archaeological discoveries was followed by the nightmare of World War I. The Louvre's masterpieces were safely stored, and donations all but ceased, except for a few major bequests such as the Baron Schlichting's. A few opportune acquisitions were also made at this time, most notably at the sale of Degas' atelier in 1917.

The return of peacetime was celebrated by the Louvre with the purchase in 1919 of Delacroix's *Death of Sardanapalus.* Peace was short-lived, however, and in 1939 the museum's masterpieces were once more taken into hiding. As the Germans advanced towards Paris, the *Venus de Milo,* the *Mona Lisa,* and *The Raft of the Medusa* were carried away to safety at Chambord and later to more discreet hiding places. Throughout this troubled period and during the post-war years, the Louvre made no investments in art. History has often shown that major acquisitions programmes depend on the state of health of the nation and that economic expansion is necessary for the development of prestigious artistic projects, and the second half of the 20th century would seem to confirm this theory: the volume of acquisitions has followed the economic situation. Furthermore, the quantity of truly exceptional works on the international art market has diminished, and those that are available are extremely expensive due to intense competition from major museums. For these reasons, most works are now acquired in lieu of death duties or as bequests or donations (such as the 3,500 pieces from the De Clerq-Boisgelin collection, acquired by the Department of Antiquities in 1967). Today, neither public funds nor private donations suffice to make outright purchases. In 1988, Georges de La Tour's *Saint Thomas* was purchased by national subscription, which would have seemed incredible a few years earlier.

Antiquities

Oriental Antiquities. Egyptian Antiquities. Greek, Etruscan, and Roman Antiquities.

The section of the Louvre devoted to Antiquities is divided into Oriental Antiquities; Egyptian Antiquities; and Greek, Etruscan, and Roman Antiquities.

The Department of Oriental Antiquities

Located in the Richelieu and Sully wings of the Louvre, the Department of Oriental Antiquities grew out of the earlier Assyrian Museum, inaugurated in 1847, following Paul-Émile Botta's archaeological excavations at Khorsabad.

The collections, which are entirely devoted to the ancient Near and Middle East, are regarded as among the richest in the world. The department is divided into three major geographical areas: Mesopotamia, Iran, and the countries of the Levant. An additional division devoted to Islamic arts is attached to the department.

Some of the Mesopotamian objects exhibited here go back to the archaic period, such as a small painted terracotta *Figurine of a Naked Woman (circa* 4500 BC) from Northern Syria and the *Sumerian Tablets (circa* 3000 BC), which are covered with inscriptions dating from the birth of writing. The great Mesopotamian civilisations and dynasties are well represented, with both smaller works such as *Gudea with a Spurting Vase (circa* 2150 BC) and monumental sculptures expressing the power of the Assyrian monarchs, such as the *Winged Bulls* in the Cour Khorsabad.

The section devoted to the Levant contains a remarkable collection of works illustrating Mediterranean civilisations: Cyprus is represented by a *Fertility Idol* dating from the 4th millennium, and the Phoenician coast by a *Fertility Goddess* taming wild animals (13th-14th centuries BC). Punic civilisation, inland Syria, and the Palestinian region are also represented: a *Male Statuette (circa* 3500) testifies to the excellence of early Palestinian craftsmanship.

The Iranian section includes works from the archaic period, represented by several terracotta *Vases from Susa (circa* 4000 BC) with highly stylised decorations; later periods are represented by a stunning *Composite Statuette* (2nd millennium) of a princess in a 'crinoline' skirt, which was found in Bactria (present-day Northern Afghanistan), and a polychrome unbaked clay *Funerary Head* depicting an Elamite. Ancient Persia is magnificently represented by the glazed brick *Archers of Darius I* from his palace at Susa.

The section devoted to Islamic Arts covers a geographical area extending from Spain to India, excluding the North African countries. It forms a separate section within the Department of Oriental Antiquities. The collection spans the periods from the dynasty of the Umayyads at the beginning of the Hegira (AD 622, first year of the Muslim era) to the Ottomans and Iran in the modern period. It includes Muslim Europe and the caliphate of Cordoba. The pieces on show, whatever their medium –ceramics, pottery, metalwork, glassware, rugs, and textiles– testify to an art that emphasised the demands of colour and decoration. Magnificently stylised geometric decorations, as well as –at least among objects designed for princely use– animal and human forms can be seen in the collection.

Egyptian Antiquities

The Department of Egyptian Antiquities, in the Sully Wing, was created by Champollion in 1826. At that time, ancient Egyptian civilisation was little known –its discovery by Europeans dates to the period of Napoleon's Egyptian military campaigns, beginning in 1798. Since then, the finds from archaeological excavations have continued to enrich the Louvre, making its collection one of the largest in the world outside Egypt.

Apart from the rooms reserved for monumental works such as *The Large Sphinx (circa* 2000 BC), found at Tanis, or *Akhhetep's Mastaba* from Sakkara *(circa* 2500 BC), the collections are displayed in chronological order.

Early Pharaonic Egypt is represented by the *Dagger from Guebel el-Arak,* with its finely carved ivory handle, and the disturbingly sober *Stele of the Serpent King,* both dating from the end of the 4th millennium.

The Old Kingdom *(circa* 2700-2200 BC) is represented by the famous painted limestone *Seated Scribe,* discovered in the cemetery at Sakkara, and the handsome interlaced couple, also painted on limestone, representing *Raherka and Merseankh.*

The Middle Kingdom (2060-1780 BC) is known for its gold work and statues. The latter include a strikingly elegant painted wooden statuette depicting a young *Gift Bearer* and a small schist statuette of *King Amenemhat III,* with its finely realistic features.

The New Kingdom *(circa* 1580-1080 BC) presided over an era of prosperity and splendour, and the Louvre possesses many excellent pieces from this time, including *The Goddess Sekhmet,* endowed with a lioness's head on a female body; the painted sandstone group representing *Senynefer and Hatchepsout;* and the finely chiselled *Torso* from the Amarnian period, believed to depict Nefertiti.

The Third Intermediate Period to the Last Dynasties *(circa* 1080-333 BC). During this period, Egyptian civilisation had entered a gradual decline, but bronze work, of which the Louvre possesses several excellent examples, was in its golden age. Notable bronzes from this period include a large statue of *The God Horus* and a *Seated Cat,* a zoomorphic representation of the goddess Bastet.

Egypt under Greek and Roman domination (333 BC -4th century AD). The period from Ptolemy's rule to that of

Augustus offers some striking examples of the fusion between the newly imported forms brought by the occupiers and the traditional techniques and subject matter of the local population. The Greek-influenced *Body of Isis* is a case in point.

Coptic Egypt (from 4th century AD). Referring both to a community and to Egyptian Christian practice, the term 'Copt' designates a specific art and culture. Examples of Coptic art at the Louvre include the Byzantine-influenced *Christ and the Abbott Mena* and numerous textiles with highly characteristic patterns, for which the Copts are justly renowned. More than 30,000 examples of textiles have been discovered to date.

The Department of Greek, Etruscan, and Roman Antiquities

The Department of Greek, Etruscan, and Roman Antiquities constitutes one of the Louvre's earliest collections—its first works date back to François I. Major collections such as that belonging to Cardinal Mazarin were later added to it. The first Museum of Antiquities was opened at the Louvre in 1800. The department is now housed in the Sully and Denon wings.

ANCIENT GREECE. Works exhibited in this section span the centuries from the Prehellenic age to the Hellenic golden age.

The Prehellenic age is represented by objects from different Aegean civilisations, notably a *Female Head (circa* 2700-2400 BC) from one of the islands of the Cyclades; its purity of form may be seen as an inspiration for contemporary sculpture.

Archaic Greece *(circa* 750-500 BC) hosted the first Olympic competition (776 BC). It is represented by jewellery, black-figured amphorae, and such striking works as a *Female Statue* from Samos, and a *Head of a Horseman (the Rampin Rider)* –whose body is in the Museum of the Acropolis in Athens– both of which seem to prefigure the coming period of great Classical sculpture.

Classical Greece *(circa* 500-330 BC) witnessed a period of political and artistic renewal. Examples of Classic Greek art include a marble *Masculine Torso* found at Miletos, the bronze *Piombino Apollo,* and bas-relief carvings such as the magnificent *Plaque from the Parthenon Frieze,* depicting a Panathenaic procession.

The Hellenistic world *(circa* 324-31 BC) of Alexander of Macedon spread Greek culture as far as India. Although artists still looked to Athens, Hellenistic art was subject to many influences. Several masterpieces were produced during this time, including *The Winged Victory of Samothrace* and the *Venus de Milo.*

THE ETRUSCANS AND THE ROMANS. Etruscan and Roman

Antiquities are exhibited in chronological order, beginning with the birth of Etruscan art and civilisation, and followed by the rise of Rome as a political and military power through its decline in the fifth century. A major part of the collection is displayed in Anne of Austria's luxurious summer apartments, on the ground floor of the Petite Galerie.

Etruscan civilisation (7th-5th century BC) is well represented at the Louvre, thanks in part to the Campana collection, acquired in 1861. Renowned as goldsmiths, bronze workers, and potters, the Etruscans have left many magnificent works, including the painted terracotta *Sarcophagus of a Married Couple* (6th century) and the exquisite bronze *Candelabra* (5th century), depicting a charming female dancer.

Ancient Rome till the reign of Augustus (3rd century BC - 1st century AD). Rome dominated the Italian peninsula until the 3rd century BC, but it did not develop its own artistic style until the 1st century. At first strongly influenced by Hellenism –as is illustrated by a marble statue of *Marcellus* and the fragment of the Altar of Peace known as *The Imperial Procession*– Roman art would come into its own with more intimate works such as the magnificent basalt *Portrait of Livia.* The Louvre possesses several fragments of frescoes from Pompeii, which was destroyed in the 1st century.

Imperial art (2nd century AD) was the fruit of the golden age of Roman culture. During this period, major monuments were erected all over the empire; they are celebrated for their impressive statues –witness the superb painted bronze bust of the Emperor Hadrian. The Roman provinces also produced significant works such *The Judgement of Paris,* a mosaic from Antioch (Turkey) that once decorated the floor of a Roman villa. Imperial art was often strongly marked by local traditions as it came into contact with Greece, Egypt, and Asia.

43

Oriental Antiquities

ALTHOUGH GREAT DIVERSITY can be seen among the traditional crafts of the civilisations represented in the Department of Oriental Antiquities, they possess certain common characteristics due primarily to economic and cultural exchanges. Throughout the three geographic areas represented in the department –Mesopotamia, the Levant, and Iran– art played the same role as the servant of religion and the sovereign. At the beginning of the 3rd millennium, urbanised societies emerged in these three large areas.

MESOPOTAMIA covered an area between the Levant and Iran, corresponding to modern-day Iraq, which was settled by the Sumerians around 3000 BC. They introduced sculpture, architecture, and writing, and gave birth to one of the most brilliant civilisations the world has ever seen. For nearly two centuries, the Sumerians dominated the region with their city-state organisation. But at the beginning of the 2nd millennium, peace was disrupted by a series of conflicts that would give rise to several kingdoms, notably Babylon, which was founded by the Amorites and later overthrown by the Kassites.

THE LEVANT comprised the countries of the eastern Mediterranean. A strategic region, it was made up of small scattered kingdoms dependent on their powerful neighbours–the Egyptians to the South and the Hittites to the North. Around 1200 BC, both powers were weakened by invasions, enabling the inhabitants of the Phoenician shores to increase their maritime dominance. Inland, the Aramaeans established independent kingdoms; one of these, Damascus, would form alliances for a time with the kingdoms of Israel, Moab, and Judaea against the growing Assyrian threat.

IRAN originated in 2500 BC in Elam, in the western part of the country near the Mesopotamian border. The Elamites were dependent on their more powerful neighbours and were often shaken by their political upheavals.

THE REGION OF THE NEAR AND MIDDLE EAST saw the rise of several empires, beginning in the ninth century BC. The Assyrians first settled in Mesopotamia, but soon their commercial and military activities took them from the Persian Gulf to the Mediterranean. Their empire collapsed around 615 BC, with the Babylonian renaissance.

THE PERSIANS, who had settled near Elam around 700 BC, also dreamt of expansion. In 480 BC, their empire spread from the Indus Valley to Libya.

A century later, Alexander the Great, then aged twenty, would conquer them. The historian Élie Faure writes: 'When Alexander reached the threshold of their palaces, his military convoy followed by ageing vanquished peoples, he stood as a symbol of ancient civilisations wandering in search of their scattered energy.'

Gudea with a Spurting Vase

Tello, formerly Girsu (Iraq), Neo-Sumerian period, circa 2150 BC / Calcite.

Gudea, Prince of Lagash, holds a sacred vase against his body; from it spurt two fish-laden streams of water that trickle down his body. This symbol of fertility is generally an attribute of divinities, rarely –as here– of a sovereign.

Fertility Goddess

Minet el-Beida, formerly Ugarit (Syria), 13th-14th century BC / Ivory.

The cover of a cosmetic box, depicting a goddess taming wild nature. The ivory carvings are highly characteristic
of Phoenician craftsmanship, but Aegean stylistic influences may be detected in the treatment of the goddess,
while Mesopotamian influences are evident in the two ibexes.

Assyrian Winged Bull from the Palace of King Sargon II

Khorsabad (Iraq),
721-705 BC / Gypsum.

The gates of the Palace of Sargon were guarded by a pair of winged bulls, protective spirits and guardians of the world. The horn tiara is an attribute of divinity. The bull is represented with five legs so as to appear in a static position when seen from the front and in motion when seen in profile.

Taureau ailé à face humaine
battant l'entrée d'une porte du palais de SARGON (VIIIᵉ siècle)

Fragment of the frieze of The Archers of Darius I

Susa (Iran), circa 500 BC / Glazed bricks.

The palace that Darius I, King of Persia, built at Susa was an architectural masterpiece of great elegance.
The frieze shown here is an example of the magnificent bas-reliefs that decorated the palace. The archers
of the royal guard are depicted in ceremonial dress rather than in battle gear.

Islamic art
Cup with a Falconer on Horseback

Iran, late 12th-early 13th centuries / Siliceous ceramic with over-glaze painted decoration,
embellished with gold and metal lustre.

This beautiful cup, with its elegant drawing, exquisite colours –closely related to the art of the miniature– and varied
techniques, dates from the golden age of Iranian pottery. The iconography shows that the representation of human
figures as part of decoration was not prohibited by the Koran, as is commonly maintained.

Egyptian Antiquities

THE NUMEROUS REMAINS from the 4th millennium testify to the existence of a highly developed culture that produced crafts of exceptional quality, but Egypt can only be said to have become a historical entity in 3100 BC, when the first Pharaonic dynasties emerged and united the kingdoms of the North and South. Writing also appeared at this time.

THE OLD KINGDOM was founded in 2700 BC and was followed by a period of consolidation of royal power, as exemplified by the construction of the pyramids at Giza and the colossal Great Sphinx –with the features of Pharaoh Khephren– who still stands guard over his necropolis. The Louvre's monumental *Large Sphinx* also testifies to the pharaoh's growing power. It is a magnificent specimen with finely chiselled details and concise volumes that serve to create a harmonious whole.

AN INTERMEDIATE PERIOD of political upheaval and confusion began in 2200 BC and came to an end in 2060 BC with the emergence of the Middle Kingdom. Artistic representations became less hieratic and more human and expressive. At this time, Egypt spread its political influence to the south, as well as to Phoenicia and Palestine. The monarchy was fragile, however, and around 1780 BC the Hyksos invaded from the east.

AROUND 1580 BC, the Hyksos were expelled and centralised power restored, permitting the foundation of the New Kingdom. This period was dominated by an expansionist policy, especially towards the east, and was marked by great rulers like Amenophis III and Ramses II, who ushered in the kingdom's golden age. The arts flourished, with painting, sculpture, and bas-relief carving reaching a peak of refinement and elegance. The artistic expression of political power, however, was first and foremost seen in architecture: the temples at El Karnak and Luxor, the tombs of the Valley of the Kings, and the prodigious treasures of Tutankhamen all date from the New Kingdom.

FROM 1080 BC, the New Kingdom began to decline. A period of political anarchy was followed by a long period of suffering caused by numerous invasions: around 700 BC, the Kuchites invaded from the south, then around 660 BC the Assyrians came from the East, followed by the Persians in 525 BC. Finally, in 333 BC, Alexander the Great had himself proclaimed son of the god Amon and ruler of Egypt.

AFTERWARD, THE KINGDOM was ruled by Ptolemy I; his dynasty came to an end with Queen Cleopatra. In 27 BC, Augustus rode into Alexandria, and Egypt became a Roman province.

BY THE TIMES THE ARABS conquered Egypt in AD 642, the country had been completely Christianised.

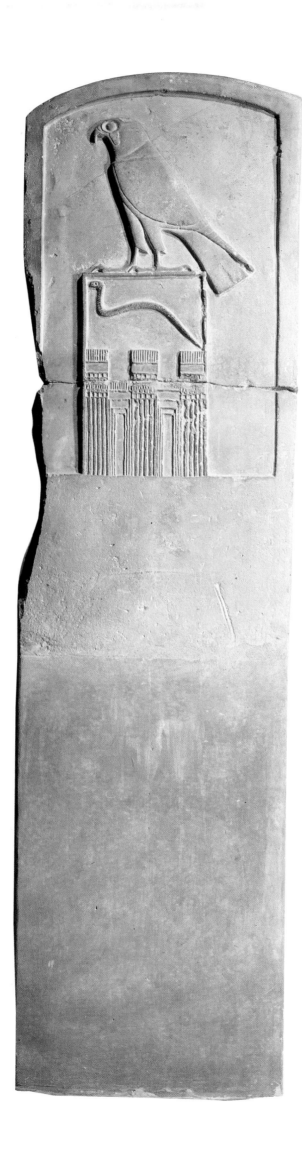

49

Stele of Djet, the Serpent King

Abydos (Egypt), *circa* 3100 BC. Limestone.

This remarkably elegant stele with finely austere carving dates from early Pharaonic Egypt and was found in the tomb of the Serpent King, the third king of the 1st Dynasty. He is represented by Horus, the falcon god of Egyptian royalty. The stele measures 1.50 metres (5 feet) in height.

50

The Large Sphinx

Tanis (Nile Delta), circa 2000 BC (Middle Kingdom) / Pink granite.

A pharaoh with a lion's body, the sphinx symbolises power and protection. In Egyptian religious architecture,
it is the guardian of sanctuaries and sacred alleys. From the 2nd millennium, sphinxes spread throughout Asia and,
later, to Greece, where they were transformed into cruel and enigmatic monsters.

*'We perceive all grand styles
as symbols of a fundamental relations
hip between humanity and the universe,
between a civilisation and the value
it regards as supreme: with its gods.'
André Malraux,
Le Musée Imaginaire, 1965.*

The Seated Scribe

Sakkara (Egypt), circa 2620-2350 BC. (Old Kingdom) / Painted limestone.

Only members of the highest levels of society knew how to read and write because these skills took so long to learn.
In the hierarchy of the scribe's profession, the top level was held by those who were attached to a temple
or who served the sovereign.

*'I love the marriage in Egyptian art
of painting and sculpture—
the detachment, the resonance.'
Zao Wou-ki,
Les Dialogues du Louvre, 1991.*

Senynefer and Hatchepsout

Circa 1410 BC (New Kingdom) / Painted sandstone.

The statues shown here are highly realistic. Their purpose in representing the dead is to perpetuate their presence
and their memory. They do not symbolise the dead; they duplicate them.

53

**Colossus of
Amenhotep IV
(Akhenaton)**

East of Karnak (Egypt)
Circa 1365-1349 BC.
(New Kingdom)
Painted sandstone.

Amenhotep IV, Queen
Nefertiti's husband,
is shown in the position
of the god Osiris, with his
arms crossed over his chest.
Also known as Akhenaton,
'the Servant of the Solar
Orb', this mystical ruler
turned Egypt towards a
monotheistic cult of the
sun, represented as the god
Aton. A poem written by
Amenhotep IV provided
inspiration for the *Psalms*
of the Old Testament.

'The works of the past that I find to resemble reality most closely are those that are generally thought to be the furthest from it —I mean the arts of different styles: Chaldea, Egypt, Byzantium, El Faiyum, Chinese objects, Christian miniatures of the High Middle Ages.'
Alberto Giacometti,
Les Dialogues du Louvre, *1991.*

Mortuary Mask of a Woman

Antinoe (Egypt), early 3rd century AD / Painted plaster.

After the collapse of the great Egyptian empire, Greek and Roman rule would force very different cultures to confront one another. This death mask is a good illustration of the adoption of an Egyptian funeral rite (the mummification and representation of the dead) by the Romans.

Christ and Abbot Mena

Baouit (Egypt), 6th century AD (Coptic Egypt) / Distemper on wood.

Christ places a protective arm on the shoulder of Abbot Mena, head of the Monastery of Saint Apollo in the village
of Baouit. In his left hand, Christ holds a holy book decorated in Byzantine style. While the Byzantine influence
is present, the Coptic style is well illustrated by the treatment of the characters' faces
and in the simplified folds of their garments.

Greek Antiquities

ORIGINATING IN THE AEGEAN, the civilisations of the Mediterranean basin flourished at the meeting point of several cultures. The Romans brought unity to the region and regarded the Mediterranean as the *mare nostrum*.

THE HELLENIC WORLD emerged during the 3rd millennium from several civilisations settled on the shores of the Aegean Sea, including Thessaly to the north of continental Greece; the Cyclades in the Aegean Sea; Crete, between Rhodes and Cythera; and, in the Peloponnese, Mycenae –famed in legend as the home of Agamemnon– the heartland and final stage in the development of Hellenism.

MYCENAEAN CIVILISATION disappeared around 1000 BC, overcome by Dorian invaders from central Greece. With them began the Geometric period, which took its name from the motifs used as decoration by the Dorians. During the coming centuries of relative obscurity, vast migrations took place throughout the Aegean world, which would be greatly enriched by contacts with Asia. The Greek *polis* emerged at this time.

THE ARCHAIC PERIOD, which began around 750 BC, was marked by several tyrants and legislators. Maritime trade and intense colonialisation favoured the adoption by Greek art of Oriental motifs. The arts flourished at this time: sculpture emerged as a major form, the temples of Paestum and Delphi were constructed, and black-figured and, later, red-figured pottery entered a golden age in the 6th century.

THE CLASSICAL PERIOD began around 500 BC, following the Athenian defeat of the Persian invaders. It was the age of the great philosophers and the construction of the Acropolis. Sculpture aimed at realism –often idealised– which is apparent in the fluid movement of the bodies and drapery, as well as in the facial expressions. The relative peace and prosperity of the Classical Age were disrupted by the Peloponnesian War between Sparta and Athens, which ended in the defeat of the Athenian empire.

AROUND 330 BC, Greece, which had so far successfully held the Persians at bay, fell partially under the rule of Philip of Macedon. The Macedonian era was characterised by expansion into Asia. It was left to Alexander the Great (who died in 323 BC) to fulfil the wildest expansionist hopes. In unifying an empire that extended from Greece to the western flanks of India, he enabled Greek culture to penetrate as far as the great cities of the East.

ROMAN EXPANSIONISM dates from the 2nd century BC. The Romans made Greece a Roman province, while assimilating Greek culture, which thus continued to profoundly influence the Roman world.

Female Head

Amorgos?, circa 2700-2400 BC / Marble.

Little is known about this statue, which probably served a religious function.
Its pure form shows great sensitivity and is characteristic
of the Cycladean art of the Aegean.

'The Greek female nude suggests voluptuousness
because it has been freed of sacred paralysis [...]
But when we cease to look at it with Christian eyes,
when we compare it, not to a Gothic nude but to
an Indian nude, our point of view changes
immediately: its eroticism evaporates, we discover
that it radiates freedom, and that its full forms
secretly wear the draperies of the Victories.'
André Malraux,
Le Musée Imaginaire, *1965.*

Winged Victory of Samothrace

Samothrace, *circa* 190 BC / Marble and limestone.

This marble figure stood on the prow of a ship carved
in limestone that served to commemorate a now
unknown naval victory. The right wing is a plaster
reconstruction. The statue's right hand, which was
found in 1950, is housed in the Louvre.

Statue of Aphrodite,
known as
'Venus de Milo'

Melos, *circa* 100 BC /
Marble.

One of the most famous
works in the Louvre, this
statue of Aphrodite was
found on the island of
Melos (Milo) in the
Cyclades. It illustrates the
return to classicism that
occurred between the 2nd
and 1st centuries BC.

GREEK AND PHOENICIAN colonisers played a major role
in the cultural development of the Italian peninsula.
The Etruscans were alone among the peoples of the
peninsula to give birth to an original pre-Roman
culture receptive to both Greek and Eastern influences,
as is illustrated by their excellent craftsmanship. At the
beginning of the 6th century BC, they founded a
kingdom in Rome, marking the birth of the city.
Expelled from Rome around 475 BC, they retained
several of their city-states, which were gradually
Romanised.

FOLLOWING THE DEPARTURE of the Etruscan rulers, the
patricians, the Roman aristocracy, took over the city.
They based their new power on a republican
constitution and proceeded to annex other regions of
the peninsula. By the dawn of the 3rd century, Rome
ruled all of Italy and began to cast its acquisitive eye on
the Mediterranean basin: after Carthage, Greece was
annexed in 146 BC, then the kingdom of Pergamum,
marking the first stride towards the East. In 46 BC,
Julius Caesar took power and ruled as dictator. At his
death, the Republic disintegrated. Augustus established
the Roman Empire in 27 BC, by which time the
Mediterranean shores were completely under Roman
domination. The period of Augustan rule was
characterised by the *pax romana,* during which the arts
and intellectual thought flourished in an unprecedented
manner, giving birth to a new Roman culture that was a
synthesis of Classical Greek culture and the new Latin
civilisation.

THE DEATH OF AUGUSTUS in AD 14 was followed by a
troubled period, after which the dynasty of the
Antonines (AD 96-192) came to power. Under the
Antonine rulers –who included Trajan, Hadrian, and
Marcus Aurelius– the Roman Empire reached its peak,
but in the field of art, the Classical Augustan ideal gave
way to a more academic style. The empire was
gradually weakened by numerous internal contradictions of a social and intellectual order, which led to a
period of outright chaos in the 190's. Imperial order
and unity were restored with difficulty in 268. Emperor
Theodosius imposed Christianity in 379, but when he
died, his sons divided the empire into East and West.
In 410, the Visigoths pillaged Rome. The Western
Roman Empire collapsed in 476; the Eastern –or
Byzantine– Empire survived until 1453.

Roman and Etruscan Antiquities

'The priest rules. Forms are enclosed in tombs.
The sculpture of sarcophagi [...],
the frescoes of funerary rooms
that tell of sacrifices and throat-slitting–
theirs is a fanatical,
superstitious, and tormented art.'
Élie Faure,
L'Art Antique, *1921.*

Sarcophagus of a Married Couple

Cerveteri (Italy), 6th century BC / Terracotta.

This sarcophagus representing a couple reclining together at a banquet was found in the necropolis at Cerveteri
by the Marquis de Campana, a renowned collector who excavated there in 1845 and 1846.

'The style of Antiquity is Life itself.
Nothing is more alive, and no other style
in the world has rendered, or been able to render,
Life as it has.'
Rodin,
Le Musée, *1904.*

Portrait of Hadrian

Second quarter of the 2nd century AD / Bronze.

Trajan's adopted son, Hadrian, was Roman emperor from AD 117 to 138.

Portrait of Livia, wife of Emperor Augustus

Circa 30 BC / Basalt.

Roman sculptors developed their art in two main areas:
historical bas-reliefs and portraits.
This portrait of Livia illustrates their preference for austere Classicism.

The Judgement of Paris

Antioch (Turkey), circa AD 115 / Mosaic in marble, limestone, and glass paste.

The mosaic shown here decorated the floor of a Roman villa in Antioch. It is an example of the great artistic quality
of works produced in some of the southern provinces of the Roman Empire.

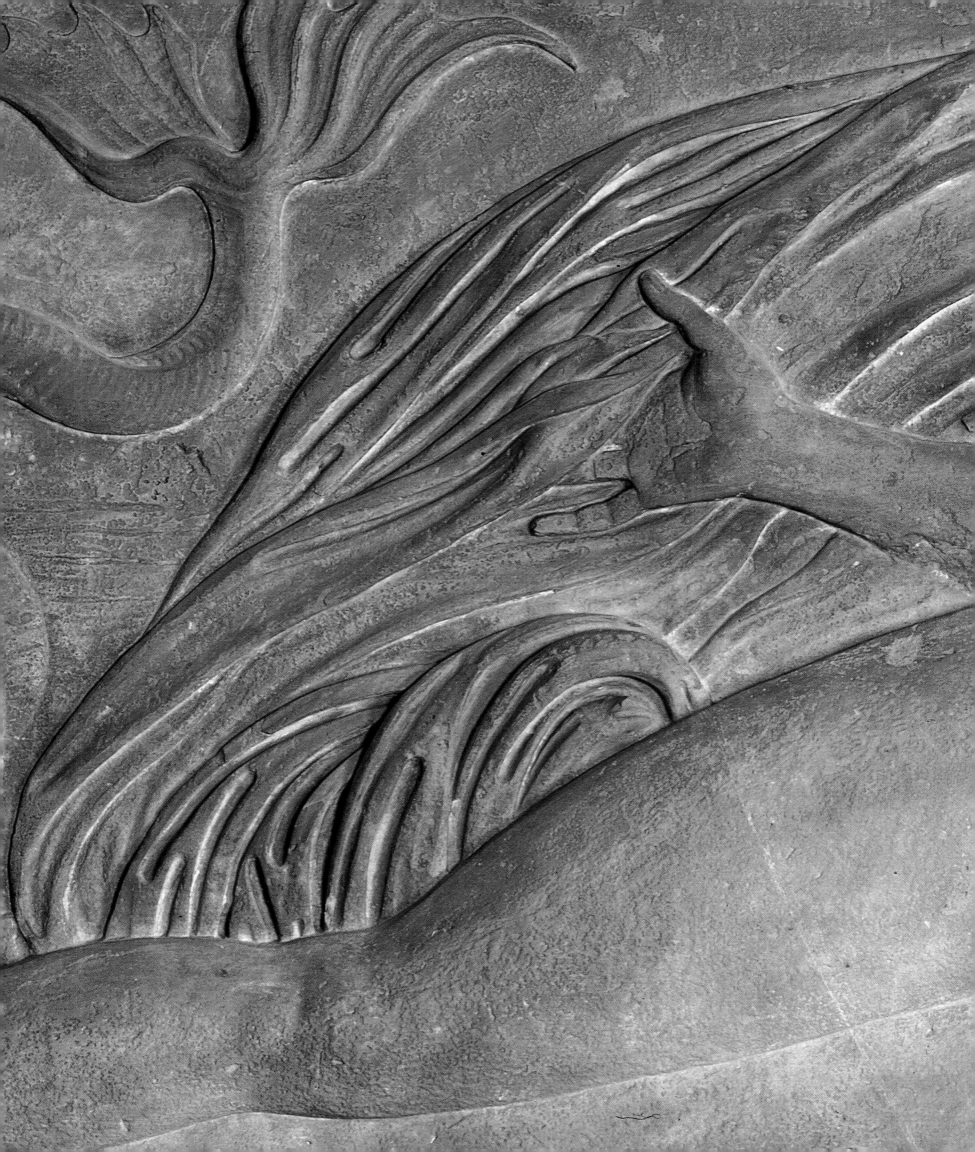

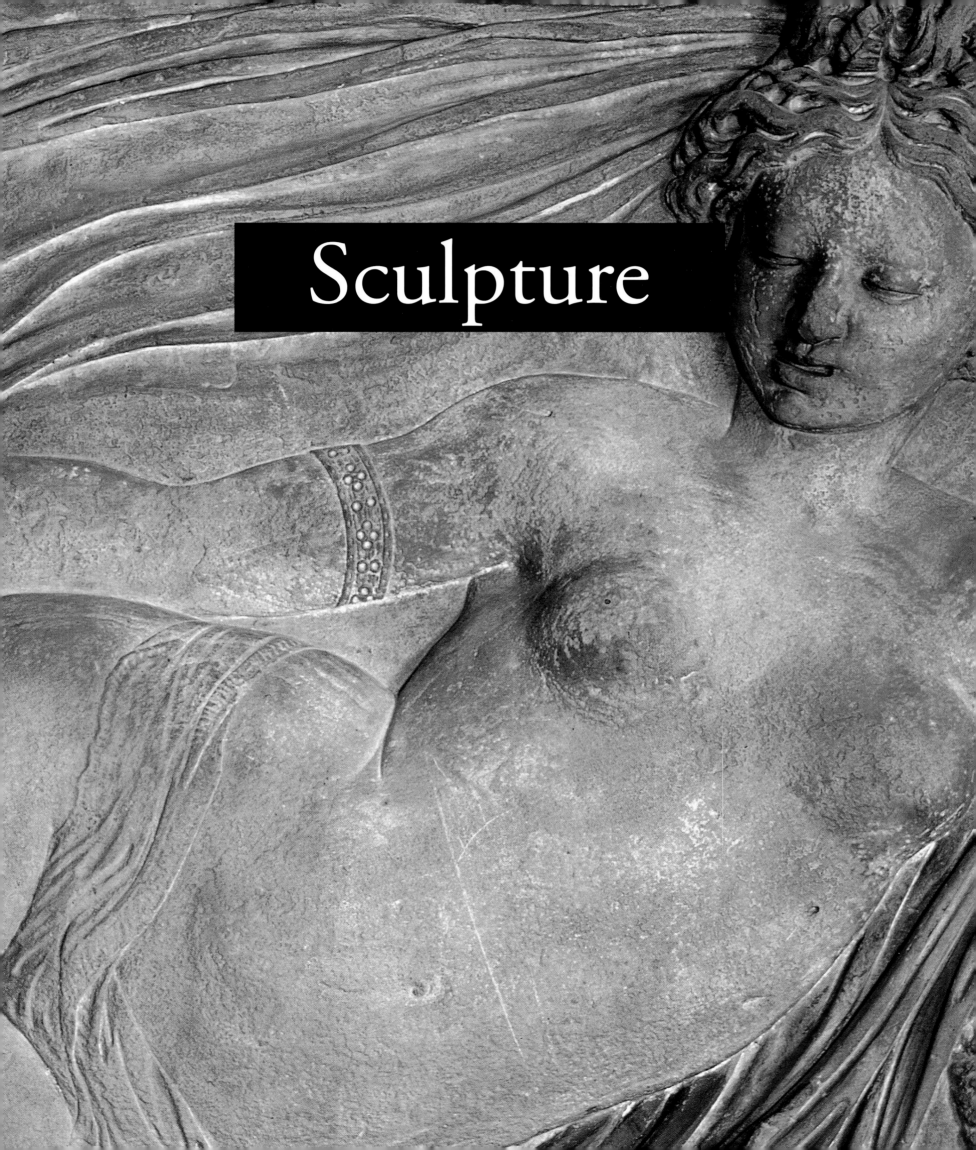

Sculpture

French and European Sculpture

The Department of Sculpture was created in 1793, when the Muséum Central des Arts was founded. It has been separate from the Department of Decorative Arts since 1871, although both departments possess small statuary. The early collection consisted only of works dating from Antiquity, with the notable exception of Michelangelo's *Slaves,* which had been confiscated from emigrants who fled the country during the Revolution and given to the Louvre in 1794. It was not till 1824 that a collection of sculptures covering the period from the Renaissance to the contemporary era found a home in the Louvre.

The collections in the Department of Sculpture have come from several sources: the Musée des Monuments Français, created by Alexander Lenoir during the Revolution to house works of art seized from religious institutions, public places, and collections belonging to emigrants; works of art that had remained in royal parks and residences; and works of admission to the Royal Academy of Painting and Sculpture. In addition, since the beginning of the 19th century, the collection has been regularly enriched by donations and an acquisitions programme.

French sculpture

French sculpture, located in the Richelieu Wing of the Louvre, offers a complete overview of the period, from the High Middle Ages to about 1850.

Romanesque sculpture (11th-12th centuries), essentially religious in nature, is represented by some powerful works: a beautifully decorated eleventh-century Merovingian marble capital depicting *Daniel and the Lions,* and a polychrome wooden *Descent from the Cross,* formerly in the Courajod collection.

Gothic sculpture (12th-15th centuries) is richly represented by works in different media and styles. Among the most striking are a relief fragment of the rood-screen from Chartres Cathedral depicting *The Angel Dictating to Saint Matthew the Evangelist,* which is both austerely beautiful and moving; the statue of *Charles V,* believed to be from the southern façade of the Château du Louvre (the statue is visible in one of the scenes depicted in the illuminated manuscript *The Very Rich Hours* of the Duc de Berry); and the *Tomb of Philippe Pot,* which eloquently represents the art of funerary statuary.

The Renaissance (15th-16th centuries) spread Italian culture beyond its borders and took on many different forms of expression. One of the earliest works of the French Renaissance is the marble relief *Saint George Fighting the*

Preceding pages

JEAN GOUJON

Nymph, Triton, and Spirits

1547-1549 / Stone (detail). From the Fontaine des Innocents, Paris.

The reliefs of Jean Goujon, characterised by great fluidity of line and extreme elegance, are among the best examples of French Renaissance sculpture. He decorated Lescot's façades for the Louvre and executed the caryatids in the ground-floor area.

Dragon, executed by Michel Colombe. Other notable French Renaissance works include Jean Goujon's emblematic reliefs, with their highly elegant, sinuous lines, as illustrated by his *Nymph and Putto,* and the reliefs adorning Pierre Lescot's façade in the Cour Carré of the Louvre; and the marble group depicting *The Huntress Diana* from the Château d'Anet, home of Diane de Poitiers, Henri II's mistress. At the summit of Renaissance sculpture are the works of Germain Pilon, including the elegantly Mannerist *Monument for the Heart of Henri II: The Three Graces,* executed for Henri II's funerary monument (the three Graces were designed to hold up a small casket containing the king's heart), and the poignantly affecting polychrome terracotta *Virgin of the Sorrows.*

During the 17th century, sometimes referred to as the 'Grand Siècle', the languorous style of late Mannerism persisted before a reaction set in and a new style developed that found a middle ground between a love for Antiquity and Italian Baroque influences.
The Louvre is especially well endowed with masterpieces by great artists of the 17th century. These include a small terracotta *Virgin and Child,* with the infant Christ shown holding a crown, by Jean Sarrazin, and a large marble group depicting *Fame Riding Pegasus* by Antoine Coysevox, made for the Château de Marly. Also by Coysevox is the *Bust of the Prince of Condé,* with its brilliant depiction of psychological states, also well handled by Martin Desjardins in his bust of *Pierre Mignard.*
Other sculptors deserving mention are the Augier brothers, Girardon, and the brilliant Pierre Puget, whose *Milon of Croton* would alter the direction of later French sculpture.

From 'style Rocaille' to Romanticism (18th-19th centuries). Guillaume Coustou's *Chevaux de Marly,* which replaced the earlier group by Coysevox, combined naturalism with intense dynamism in a manner typical of French Baroque art —also know as the *'style Rocaille'.* During the 1750's, the accent on greater naturalism did not exclude the development of an austerely refined style, as illustrated by Jean-Baptiste Pigalle's *Mercury Attaching his Wings* and Augustin Pajou's *Psyche Abandoned.*
The increasingly austere style would result in Neoclassicism, as illustrated by Antoine-Denis Chaudet's *Cupid,* shown playing with a butterfly and a rose. Unexpectedly, Neoclassicism in turn gave rise to the Romanticism of Jeahan Duseigneur's *Orlando Furioso* and —to a lesser extent and in a different genre— to Antoine-Louis Barye's *Lion Fighting a Serpent.*

European Sculpture

The section devoted to European sculpture, located in the Denon Wing, is made up of various collections and, while there are some major gaps, it offers a general overview of Northern European and Italian sculpture.

Germanic countries. With the exception of a 12th-century *Christ on the Cross,* the collection of sculpture from Germanic countries at the Louvre dates from the 15th century, with works such as a seated *Virgin and Child* from a Basle workshop and the polychrome marble *Virgin of the Annunciation* by Tilman Riemenschneider, master of a flourishing workshop in Würzburg. Both works illustrate Late Gothic style, as does the wooden polychrome *Saint Mary Magdalene* by the German sculptor Gregor Erhart.

The Low Countries. The exquisite 16th-century *Altarpiece of the Passion* was produced by a workshop in the Antwerp area–a region that was renowned for its altarpieces. The high-relief alabaster *Cavalry* is the work of the Flemish artist Willem van den Broek.

Italy. Most of the Italian works in the collections of the Louvre date from the 13th century, exemplified by a powerful *Descent from the Cross* from central Italy. The Quattrocento is represented by a *Virgin and Child* by Donatello, a major artist of the Italian Renaissance. The Louvre possesses two 16th-century masterpieces by Michelangelo, *The Dying Slave* and *The Bound Slave,* originally conceived for Pope Julius II's funerary monument. Also dating from the 16th century is Benvenuto Cellini's bronze relief *Nymph of Fontainebleau,* executed for the Château d'Anet.
The 17th century is represented by Bernini's marble bust of *Cardinal Richelieu,* which was seized from the Chapterhouse of the Cathedral of Notre-Dame during the Revolution. Late 18th-and early 19th-century sculpture was greatly influenced by Antonio Canova, whose *Eros and Psyche* demonstrates that Neoclassicism need not preclude the depiction of the emotions.

French Sculpture

IN THE 11TH CENTURY, stable feudal power and an atmosphere of religious fervour combined to create the necessary climate for the development of Romanesque art, the first major style produced by Western Christianity. Religious buildings were erected all over the country, and sculpture was required to submit to architectural constraints.

IN THE SECOND HALF OF THE 12TH CENTURY, the austere poignancy and robust horizontals of Romanesque architecture were succeeded by the soaring verticality of Gothic, which may be seen both as an affirmation of royal power and an expression of spiritual fervour. While appearing to seek an almost Classical equilibrium, Gothic sculpture was characterised by eloquent facial expressions, supple forms, and fluid drapery. It developed subtle variations in the different parts of France in which it flourished: Burgundy, Languedoc, and the Loire Valley.

DURING THE RENAISSANCE, many Italian artists worked in France and helped spread the new ideals of moderation and clarity that French artists would adapt to their own national tradition. Germain Pilon gave the new style a highly refined expression without abandoning the constraints of realistic portraiture. He was also capable of expressing great pathos, as can be seen in works such as *The Virgin of the Sorrows.*

IN THE 17TH CENTURY, a fascination with Classical Antiquity and an attraction for the Italian Baroque gave rise to a new French school that combined elegance with austerity. Among the artists active at this time, Coysevox is remembered for his sometimes profoundly disturbing depictions of psychological states; while Puget's lyricism is credited with giving rise to Cézanne's credo: 'Strength and distinction.'

IN THE 18TH CENTURY, under the Regency, a more exuberant style known as *'Rocaille'* flourished for a time. But scarcely had it established itself in the 1750's than it was replaced by a return to Classicism and a fashionable penchant for anything 'natural'.

NEOCLASSICISM emerged shortly before the Revolution and became the official style of the Empire. An austere, Spartan style, it produced rigorous sculptural forms, which despite their apparent iciness could express great subtlety. The works of some Neoclassical artists show that they were receptive to the Romantic quest for greater emotional expression.

Descent from the Cross

Second quarter of the 12th century / Wood with gilt and polychrome traces.

Central figure from a Descent *from the Cross* in Burgundian Romanesque style.

Tomb of Philippe Pot

Citeaux Abbey-Church, last quarter of the 15th century / Painted stone with gilt.

The funerary monument of the great seneschal of Burgundy. Each one of the eight mourners carries an emblazoned
shield bearing the arms of one of the deceased's titles of nobility. Although the sculpted figures do not attain
the greatness of some contemporary funerary statuary, their expressive force and powerful inspiration make
this tomb a work of great distinction.

'*The anger of a boxer, the impudence of fauns,*
You who knew how to gather the beauty of boors,
Your great heart swollen with pride, weak cowardly man,
Puget, melancholy emperor of convicts.'
Charles Baudelaire,
Les Fleurs du Mal, *1857.*

PIERRE PUGET

**Milon of Croton
Devoured by a Lion**

1682 / Marble.

Puget, who worked in
Provence and had lived in
Italy, was more receptive
than the court artists to the
full force of the Italian
Baroque style. Known for
his fiery, individualistic
personality, he wrote
to Louvois: 'I've been
nourished by great works.
When I work I'm in a rage,
and the marble trembles
before me, no matter how
large the piece.'

ANTOINE
COYSEVOX

Fame Riding Pegasus

1702 / Marble.

Executed for Marly Park,
near Versailles, *Fame*
formed a pair with
Mercury Riding Pegasus.
Coysevox executed both
monumental groups in two
years. They were later
moved to the Tuileries
Gardens and have been
installed at the Louvre
since 1986.

ANTOINE-DENIS CHAUDET

Cupid Playing with a Butterfly

1802-1817 / Marble.

Chaudet's work is characteristic of the Neoclassical movement, which spread throughout Europe at the beginning
of the 19th century. This delicate, graceful work refutes the accusation of coldness
and austerity often cited by detractors of Neoclassicism.

JAMES PRADIER

Satyr and Bacchante

1834 / Marble.

Writing about the Salon of 1846, Baudelaire declared: 'The proof that sculpture is in a pathetic state is that Monsieur
Pradier is the King of Sculptors.' Baudelaire's harsh criticism expresses the contradictions then confronting artists as
they hesitated between their Neoclassical heritage and the demands of the fiery new Romanticism. Should sculpture be
purely ornamental (Pradier took part in the great projects of the July Monarchy), or should it seek a more intimate
expression based on feelings and passions?

Italian and Northern European Sculpture

AS THE ART OF SCULPTURE DEVELOPED in the European
cultural melting pot, it followed many different directions.
When Romanesque art began to spread throughout
Europe in the 11th century, each country made its own
subtle additions and modifications to the style: the
Germanic Holy Roman Empire remained attached for a
long time to the Carolingian tradition; Italy conserved
traces of Byzantine style; and Spanish Romanesque art was
influenced by Muslim culture.

THE SAME IS TRUE of Gothic art, which flourished at
different times in the various countries. Though the
Gothic style first appeared in France during the second
half of the 12th century, it only reached Italy –via Tuscan
sculpture– a century later. Each country developed its own
current, which in turn influenced French art, before
merging around 1400 into a more unified style known
as International Gothic.

STYLISTIC MIGRATION thus kept regional styles from
hardening, but some local specialisations did develop
–witness the nearly industrial output of altarpieces during
the 15th century in Antwerp and some Rhineland cities,
from which they were shipped all over Europe.

A NEW STYLE EMERGED IN ITALY at this time. The interest
in Greek and Roman statuary, as expressed in the work of
the Florentine sculptor Donatello, exercised a major
influence. One of the artists he inspired in the following
century was Michelangelo, the archetype of the
Renaissance artist: a lonely, high-strung genius extracting
from brute matter the very essence of the human spirit.
Michelangelo would serve as a model for 16th-century
European Mannerists and for Baroque artists of the
17th century.

BERNINI, that great stage manager of Baroque scenes,
assimilated Michelangelo's dynamic forms and carried
them to a paroxysm of tortured movement. When he had
to curb his fiery talent in the execution of a portrait –as
in the cold marble of his Richelieu– he made up for it by
expressing psychological power.

FROM THE 17TH TO THE EARLY 18TH CENTURY, Baroque
art sought an increasingly close fusion of architecture and
the decorative arts. Around 1760, Baroque seemed to have
run its course. The rediscovery of Antiquity encouraged
greater austerity and paved the way for the emergence
of Neoclassicism all over Europe, thanks to such
cosmopolitan artists as the Italian Antonio Canova and
the Dane Berthel Thorwaldsen, who developed a careful
balance between elegance and sensuality.

DOMENICO
DI NICCOLÒ
DEI CHORI

**Virgin of the
Annunciation**

Siena, *circa* 1420-1430
Painted wood with gilt.

Siena was among
the most important artistic
centres in Italy.
The Gothic style
appeared late in Italy,
arriving via Tuscany,
where it was assimilated
and reinterpreted
by Sienese artists.

Annunciation

Brabant, late 15th century / Polychrome oak.

The 15th century was known for its altarpieces, which were produced in great numbers in Flemish workshops
and shipped all over Europe. Each production centre had a characteristic signature: a mallet for Brussels,
a cut-off hand for Antwerp.

'Michelangelo, area of vagueness where Hercules
And Christ figures mix, where powerful ghosts
Rise suddenly, and in the evening
Put out their fingers, ripping their shrouds...'
Charles Baudelaire,
Les Fleurs du Mal, *1857.*

MICHELANGELO BUONARROTI,
known as MICHELANGELO

The Bound Slave

Rome, 1513-1515 / Marble.

Michelangelo conceived several figures of slaves
to decorate the base of a projected mausoleum
at Saint Peter's in the Vatican for Pope Julius II.
It was never completed.
The pope is buried in a simple tomb in San Pietro
in Vincoli, where he is watched over
by Michelangelo's *Moses.*

WILLEM VAN DER BROECK, known as PALUDANO

Calvary

Alabaster.

The work of Willem van der Broeck, a Flemish artist who was born in 1530, is an example of the enormous influence
exercised by the Italian Renaissance on artists all over Europe in the fields of sculpture, painting, and music.

*'The most wonderful
virtue of all is truth,
because ultimately
it is revealed by time.'*
Gian Lorenzo Bernini

GIAN LORENZO BERNINI

Cardinal Armand du Plessis de Richelieu

Rome, 1640-1641 / Marble.

Bernini did not invent Baroque sculpture, but he is responsible for its triumphant flourishing. According
to philosopher Walter Benjamin, the Baroque style strives for an 'emblematic representation' of meaning and is not
a historical accessory. The bust of Richelieu confirms Benjamin's thought: it does not replicate the cardinal's physical
appearance, but offers instead an indestructible sense of his psychological presence.

ANTONIO CANOVA

Eros and Psyche

Rome, 1793 / Marble.

Neoclassical painting found its mentor in David, and Canova played the same role in sculpture.
Eros and Psyche, acquired by Murat in 1800, is representative of the Neoclassical style, which successfully combined
emotion and purity. In the myth illustrated here, Eros is about to revive Psyche, who has been put to sleep
by a magic perfume. Their gracefully entwined bodies seem suspended in time and space as soft shadows
play on the translucent white marble.

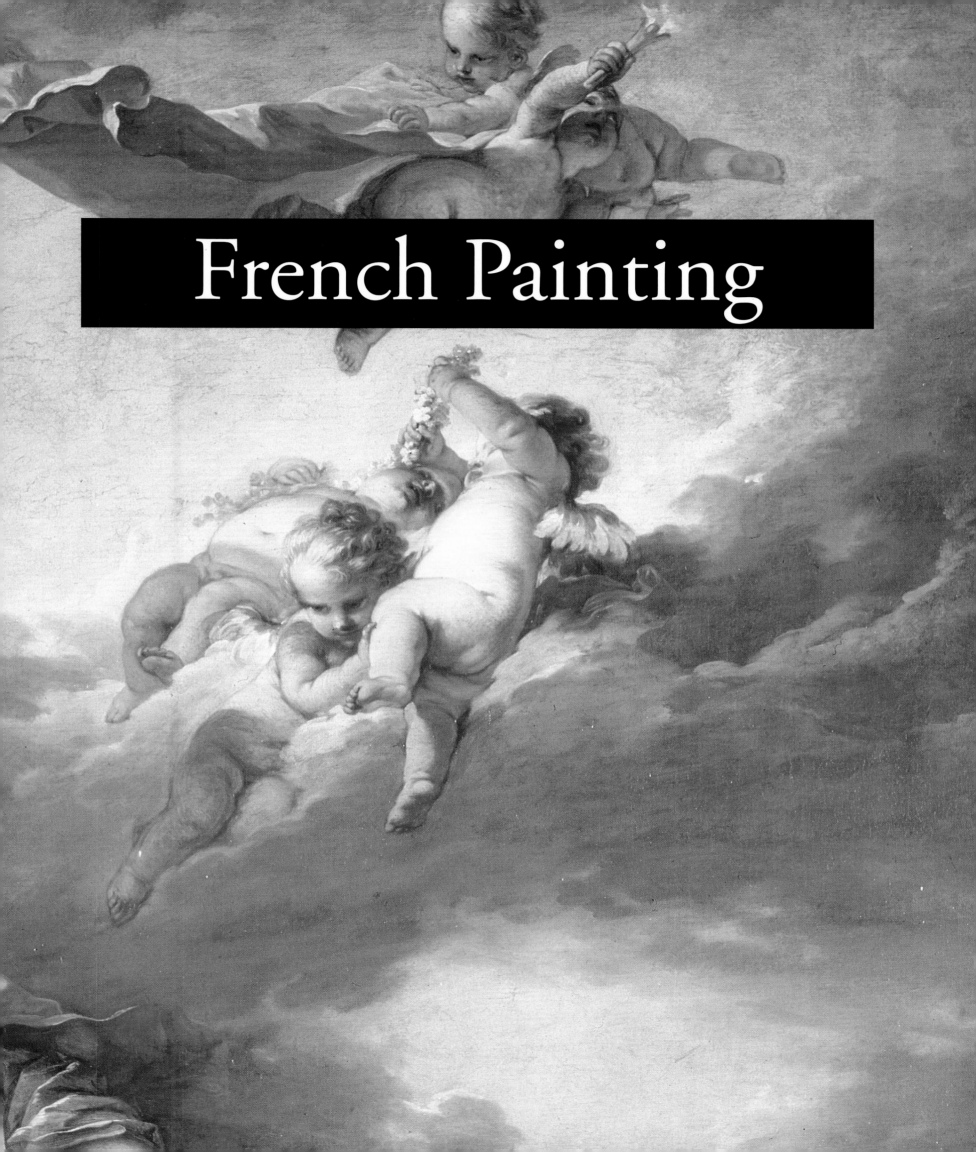

French Painting

Fourteenth- to nineteenth-century French painting

The Louvre has a collection of more than 6,000 paintings spanning nearly six centuries, more than half of which are French works. They are displayed in the Richelieu and Sully wings, except for monumental 19th-century canvasses, which hang in the Denon Wing. The preponderance of French painting is a relatively recent development in the history of the collections. An examination of the inventories of Crown possessions shows that François I neglected contemporary French artists –his portrait painted by Jean Clouet is an exception– in favour of Italian art, of which he was a fervent admirer. It was only after Louis XIV that works by French artists were acquired in significant numbers for the royal collections. These collections, which were requisitioned during the Revolution, were enriched by works from the Royal Academy, as well as by property seized from emigrants and the clergy –notably 17th-century religious paintings that had filled churches and convents. But the great period of growth for the Louvre's collections of French paintings was the 19th century, when a coherent policy of acquisitions converged with several major donations, including La Caze's excellent collection of 18th-century art, which entered the Louvre in 1869. Some of the greatest canvasses by Watteau and Chardin in the Louvre today were part of the La Caze donation. Some major donations entered the Louvre in the 20th century, including Thomy Thiéry's collection of paintings from the Barbizon school in 1902, and Moreau-Nélaton's collection of works by Corot in 1927. The Louvre's collections come to a close with works by artists who were born no later than the 1820's.

Early French Masters (14th-15th centuries) are represented by works of great quality. The portrait of *John II (the Good), King of France,* executed around 1350, is the first known easel painting and probably the earliest individual portrait painted in Europe. Other masterpieces exhibited nearby include *Christ on the Cross with the Martyrdom of St. Denis* (The Altarpiece of Saint Denis), executed in 1416 by Henri Bellechose, a painter of the Franco-Flemish school, and the very moving *Pietà of Villeneuve-lès-Avignon* of the school of Provence, dated 1455 and attributed to Enguerrand Quarton, recognised as one of the summits of religious art. Among several excellent portraits dating from the same period are two by Jean Fouquet, one depicting Charles VII and the other the Chancellor Guillaume Jouvenal des Ursins. The late 15th century, when Gothic was in its final brilliant phase, is well illustrated by the *Portrait Presumed to be of Madeleine of Burgundy, Presented by St. Madeleine* by Jean Hey, also known as the Master of Moulins.

The Renaissance (16th century) is represented by such masterpieces as the enigmatic *Eva Prima Pandora,* one of the earliest nudes in French painting, by Jean Cousin the Elder, and *Augustus and the Triburtine Sibyl* by Antoine Caron, the official painter of Catherine de' Medici.

The art of portraiture is epitomised by Jean Clouet's *François I;* while the portrait of the apothecary *Pierre Quthe* by his son François Clouet is a remarkable synthesis of Italian and Flemish influences. Three anonymous works by artists of the school of Fontainebleau also deserve mention: *Charity; Diana the Huntress,* said to represent Diane de Poitiers, and the gracefully mischievous *Gabrielle d'Estrées and One of Her Sisters,* which seems to hide an unelucidated enigma. *Ancient Sacrifice* by Toussaint Dubreuil provides a good example of the accentuated Mannerism of the second school of Fontainebleau.

The 17th century, sometimes known as the 'Grand Siècle', is richly represented by many major works illustrating the various directions taken by French painting at the time. One of these trends is exemplified by works painted by Caravaggio's followers, who had learnt from the artist in Rome how to combine realism with a powerful use of the contrast between light and shade *(chiaroscuro)*. They are represented by such works as *The Young Singer* by Claude Vignon, and the touching *Concert,* in which the artist Valentin de Boulogne revealed an independent style despite the influence of Caravaggio. Other artists who worked during the reign of Louis XIII include Nicolas Tournier, the Le Nain brothers, and Georges de La Tour, that master of night scenes who also produced same magnificent daytime works such as *The Cheat with the Ace of Diamonds,* executed around 1635. Simone Vouet, who painted the admirable *Allegory of Wealth* around 1640, abandoned the influence of Caravaggio in favour of a dazzling lyricism that would later pervade the works of the French school.

Until the 20th century, French art was greatly influenced by Nicolas Poussin, whose *Inspiration of the Poet,* bathed in golden light, seems to represent the alliance of creative power with intellectual thought. Philippe de Champaigne, a friend of Poussin's youth, reached the summit of his art with *The Ex-Voto of 1662* in which he painted his daughter Catherine next to Agnès Arnaud. Claude Gellée, known as Le Lorrain, a friend of Poussin's in his later years, is represented by several views of ports and landscapes depicting imaginary architecture, such as *The Landing of Cleopatra at Tarsus.* The next generation included artists like Charles Le Brun, who, though he was primarily known as the organiser of royal festivities, was also an excellent artist, as is demonstrated by the monumental historical compositions exhibited at the Louvre and by such works as *Chancellor Séguier,* painted in homage to his first protector. Many other artists are worthy of mention: Sébastien

Bourdon, a brilliantly versatile painter who deserves to be better known; Laurent de La Hyre, a great landscape artist; and Eustache Le Sueur, who succeeded in radiating tenderness without affectation, as can be seen in the series of panels depicting the Muses. The 'Grand Siècle' is also represented by artists who made the transition to the 18th century, including Pierre Mignard, who supplanted Le Brun in the 1680's, and painters such as La Fosse, Jouvenet, Rigaud, Largillière, and the Coypels.

The Enlightenment (18th century) produced as great a variety of styles as the 'Grand Siècle'. Watteau's *Embarkation for Cythera* and *Gilles* (also known as *Pierrot*) evoke the fragility of passing time. Chardin later reinterpreted this sense of fragility in a more serene manner in *The Buffet* and *The Ray.* Very different approaches were taken by Boucher, who favoured colourful, dizzying movement, as shown in *The Rape of Europa,* and by Fragonard, who needed fewer mythological pretexts than his predecessors to undress his figures.

Following the Regency and the reign of Louis XV, during which time artists developed a fascination with the nude, a moralising, bourgeois reaction set in. This period is well represented at the Louvre by artists such as Madame Vigée-Lebrun and Greuze; the latter, who is known for the effusive moral didacticism of *The Punishment of Filial Ingratitude,* is also the author of the allusively erotic *Broken Pitcher.*

The mid-18th century looked back to Greek and Roman Antiquity. The period is represented by Joseph-Marie Vien, the precursor of Neoclassicism, and most notably by his student, Jacques-Louis David, whose major paintings are exhibited at the Louvre: *The Oath of the Horatii,* regarded as his manifesto, and *The Lictors Bringing Brutus the Bodies of His Sons.* A new interest in landscape painting also developed at this time, represented by artists such as Valenciennes and Hubert Robert, who is remembered for his paintings of ruins.

From Romanticism to the Barbizon school (early 20th century). Both Neoclassicism and Romanticism flourished during the Empire, and imperial pomp was rivalled only by epic ardour. The Romantic school, which succeeded David and his followers, is represented at the Louvre by Géricault's *Raft of the Medusa* and his *Wounded Cuirassier,* and Delacroix's *Death of Sardanapalus, Liberty Leading the People,* and *Orphan Girl at the Cemetery,* among works by many other artists.

The early 19th century saw the development and flowering of Ingres in his many artistic incarnations: the 'bourgeois' painter of the portrait of *Louis-François Bertin,* the artist of Neoclassical purity who executed the portrait of *Made-moiselle Caroline Rivière,* and the sensual painter of *The Turkish Bath.* Chassériau learned from Ingres and Delacroix and during his brief career developed his own characteristic style, notably in *The Toilette of Esther* and *Father Dominique Lacordaire,* in which he showed his deferent affection for his model. Following in the footsteps of Valenciennes, Robert, and Michallon, 19th-century artists put landscape painting in the forefront of French art. Landscapes exhibited at the Louvre include some of the most modern works in the museum: *The Sin-le-Noble Road* and *The Church of Marissel, near Beauvais,* both by Corot, as well as numerous works by Charles Daubigny and Théodore Rousseau. Later artists are exhibited across the Seine at the Musée d'Orsay.

ENGUERRAND QUARTON

Pietà of Villeneuve-lès-Avignon

Provence, circa 1455 / Paint on wood.

An inscription from *The Lamentations of Jeremiah* runs along the border of the painting:
'All ye that pass by behold and see if there be any sorrow like unto my sorrow'.
A powerful expression of religious devotion, the *Pietà* is also a poignant depiction of human suffering.
In 1834, the painting, which was then at Villeneuve-lès-Avignon, came to the attention
of a young Inspector of Historical Monuments, Prosper Mérimée,
who later became known as a writer.
It entered the Louvre in 1905 as a gift from the Société des Amis du Louvre.

THE EMERGENCE OF THE FIRST EASEL PAINTINGS in the 14th century was a significant cultural development. Unfortunately, few of them have survived. It was not until the following century that easel painting flourished as a rival to miniature art. The earliest works were solemn, but without undue austerity. They harmoniously blended a number of different traditions: in addition to Flemish and Italian, these included the specific influences of the various French centres where the new art developed (Burgundy, Avignon, the Loire Valley, and Moulins).

SURPRISINGLY, THE DEFINITION OF A SPECIFICALLY FRENCH STYLE of a specifically French style came from Italy. The school of Fontainebleau developed in 1530, under the influence of many renowned Italian artists, including Leonardo da Vinci, and especially Rosso and Primaticcio, who worked in France during the reign of François I. As a result of the Italian influence, biblical austerity gave way to allegorical and mythological subjects; bodies were now lightly clad, draughtsmanship gained in elegance, and fresh colours made their appearance.

A HIGHLY REFINED, it made frequent use of subtle allusions and ambiguity, as well as an affected form of eroticism. In the declining years of the Renaissance, the second school of Fontainebleau adopted an exaggerated form of Mannerism, whose self-conscious rhetoric was lacking in imagination.

AT TH BEGINNING OF THE 17TH CENTURY, a new generation of young artists travelled to Italy in search of fresh inspiration. In Rome, Vouet, Valentin, and Vignon discovered the Classicism of the Carraccis, and the powerful naturalism and *chiaroscuro* of Caravaggio. Some French artists, notably Poussin and Le Lorrain, settled and worked in Rome, while many others visited the Eternal City in order to plunge into the Ancient world before returning to France to establish their careers.

UP TO A POINT, Louis XIII succeeded in his goal of stealing Italy's mantle of artistic supremacy. During his reign, the arts in France blossomed: from easel painting to decorative murals, from religious art to royal or private commissions. The newly found creative energy continued to flourish during Louis XIV's reign, which Le Brun was said to have endowed with grandeur.

ECOLE DE FONTAINEBLEAU

Diana the Huntress

Circa 1550-1560 / Oil on canvas.

This representation of Diana the huntress was doubtless painted in homage to the beauty
of Diane de Poitiers, Henri II's mistress.
The subject matter and the style –the elongated body and affected pose– were typical
of the school of Fontainebleau.

GEORGES DE LA TOUR

The Cheat with the Ace of Diamonds

Circa 1630 / Oil on canvas.

La Tour, who is here at the peak of his art, has chosen a subject that is close to the heart of Caravaggio
and his followers. But it is tempting to see in *The Cheat* more than a simple tavern scene.
The painter perhaps wished to illustrate the story of the prodigal son, represented by the young boy; the other
characters personify the vices –from left to right: gambling, wine, and lust.
The subtle exchange of glances between the other players seems to put the youth at the mercy
of the all-too-human treachery of a disillusioned world.

'The splash of red in the wine glass gives colour
to the whole painting. Without it, it doesn't exist...
What likeable faces!...
All those eyes that don't look at us.
The old woman looks inward. Such nostalgia in her eyes!'
Alberto Giacometti,
Les Dialogues du Louvre, *1991*.

LOUIS or ANTOINE LE NAIN

Peasant Family in an Interior

1642 / Oil on canvas.

The Peasant Family is not only the Le Nains' greatest 'peasant' painting, but is also the most touching because
of the intense humility with which the dignified and worn figures of the poor are depicted.
No meal has been prepared, and their attention is fully focused on the bread and wine,
which take on a religious significance.

SIMON VOUET

Allegory of Wealth

Circa 1640 / Oil on canvas.

Its full forms, bright colours, and decorative monumentality make the *Allegory of Wealth* one of Vouet's masterpieces.
When the artist returned to France in 1627 after a prolonged sojourn in Italy, he helped to renew French painting.

'Order and passion, intellect and plasticity,
experience and naiveté, Olympian equilibrium and peasant
earthiness. When confronted with form and nature,
he behaves as a poet of colour.'
André Masson, Le plaisir de peindre, *1950*.

NICOLAS POUSSIN

Inspiration of the Poet

Circa 1630 / Oil on canvas.

When Bernini visited Paris in 1665, he exclaimed before Poussin's canvas: 'It is painted and coloured
in the manner of Titian.' Both its luminosity and its colours show the influence of the Venetians.
The poet stands on the right, looking upward to heaven, the source of his inspiration. The central seated figure
is Apollo, god of music and poetry. Calliope, muse of eloquence and poetry, stands on the left.
The title of the painting is explicit, but Poussin, who claimed that he could make 'mute objects'
speak, may have been trying to show that painting could equal poetry.

'Those who said that Lorrain had not learnt
his craft could at least have added that everyone
helped themselves freely to his work.'
Auguste Renoir

CLAUDE GELLÉE, known as LE LORRAIN

The Landing of Cleopatra at Tarsus

1642 / Oil on canvas.

As is often the case with the works of Le Lorrain, this painting is part of a matched set, the other canvas being
The Consecration of David by Samuel. Together, the two works may be seen to contrast a queen's ambition with
the royal destiny of a humble young man. But although the artist used biblical and historical subject matter,
the narrative served only as a pretext for painting imaginary architecture, majestic ships with furled and
unfurled sails, and sumptuous plays of light and shade.

CHARLES LE BRUN

Chancellor Séguier

Circa 1657-1661 / Oil on canvas.

Before becoming the official organiser of royal festivities and one of the main interior decorators of royal dwellings,
Le Brun had studied under Vouet and travelled to Rome, where he had met Poussin. Séguier was his patron.
The beauty of this painting –with its subtle silver and golden hues and its Venetian sky– shows that Le Brun was not
only a painter of epic decors. Two of the figures look out at the spectator in a most unusual manner:
the powerful chancellor's look is serene, while the young squire's is gentle and timid.

*'And it is even true
that his first ideas
and his less-finished
works were often better
than the things
he wished to keep
working on, because
the ardour
of his imagination
provided enough
to satisfy the eye.'
André Félibien,*
Entretien sur les Vies
et sur les Ouvrages
des Plus Excellents
Peintres, *1679.*

SÉBASTIEN
BOURDON

**Descent
from the Cross**

Circa 1645 /
Oil on canvas.

Sometimes referred
to as the 'Proteus
of painting', Bourdon
produced a large body
of work marked
by the ardour
and zeal noted by his
contemporaries.
Such vigour and
impetuosity was bound
to appeal to Delacroix,
who made a copy of the
Descent from the Cross,
which Bourdon
had painted for the Church
of Saint Benoît in Paris.
It is typical of many
of the religious
commissions made
at the time, whether for
small works or large
altarpieces.

EUSTACHE LE SUEUR

Clio, Euterpe and Thalia

1652-1655 / Oil on wood.

Le Sueur was at first influenced by his teacher Simon Vouet, then developed his own elegant style, free of all
histrionics. He was also known as a gifted painter of religious subjects. The panel shown here, depicting the Muses of
History, Music, and Comedy, was one of a series of panels of the Muses that decorated the Hôtel Lambert in Paris.

Eighteenth- to nineteenth-century French painting

From Watteau to Romanticism

MONTESQUIEU WROTE: 'The French change their morals according to the age of their king.' The reign of Louis XIV was a period of mythological and militaristic solemnities, before it turned to quieter pursuits in the king's old age. Even before the death of the Sun King, however, the Enlightenment had already dawned.

THE NEW MOOD OF THE 18TH CENTURY is represented by Watteau, both in his richly colourful palette and fresh new subject matter revolving around 'fêtes galantes' –those graceful scenes depicting the ephemeral games of seduction of the French aristocracy. Subsequently, other artists would continue in the same vein –blending grace and elegance, poetry and sensuality– making it one of the hallmarks of French art. With Boucher, the depiction of fleeting moments of desire was replaced by libertine scenes, while his student Fragonard painted quantities of creamy white flesh in unruly poses frolicking in a chaotic tangle of sheets and emotions.

EIGHTEEN-CENTURY SOCIETY WAS AVID FOR PLEASURE: artists favoured scenes showing lavish meals and hunting parties. Portraits and landscapes were painted for their own sakes, with no excuse required. A more poetic direction was taken by Jean Siméon Chardin in his magnificent still lifes.

DISSIPATION AND VIRTUE were two conflicting aspects of the age: Fragonard and Greuze were contemporaries, and both died during the Empire. The eloquent sensuality of the former seemed in total opposition to the bourgeois didacticism of the latter, and yet by the 1770's younger artists were beginning to find both old-fashioned. They searched for new inspiration in ancient Greece and Rome: the century that had excelled in the exuberant 'Rocaille' style would now see a return to the austerity of Antiquity. Jacques-Louis David became the leader of the new school, which would give rise in the following century to such very different artists as Ingres and Delacroix.

ROMANTICISM CAN BE CREDITED with the rediscovery of landscape. Romantic landscape painting is represented by Corot, who continued the tradition of Le Lorrain and Poussin, and by the school of Barbizon, more attentive to 17th-century Flemish painting. The Louvre's collections of painting come to a close with the school of Barbizon, which foresaw the realism of Courbet and the work of the Impressionists, exhibited at the Musée d'Orsay.

'Gilles is a white innocent sun: an other-worldly presence, shown here and now. It is one of the most mysterious paintings in the world–and one of the most beautiful.'
Philippe Sollers,
Le Cavalier du Louvre, *1994.*

JEAN-ANTOINE WATTEAU

Pierrot, formerly known as **Gilles**

Circa 1718-1719 / Oil on canvas.

This painting was purchased from a bric-a-brac salesman by Vivant Denon, director of the Louvre during the First Empire. It is Watteau's only life-sized work and may have been painted as a sign for a café that the actor Belloni, who was famed for his roles as a Pierrot, had just opened near Les Halles in Paris.

'Oh, Chardin! It is not white, or red, or black
that you mix on a palette: it is the very substance
of the objects; you put air and light on the tip
of your brush and daub them on the canvas.'
Diderot,
Salon de 1763.

JEAN SIMÉON CHARDIN

The Ray

1728 / Oil on canvas.

On 25 September 1728, at the age of 28, Chardin became a member of the Royal Academy of Painting and Sculpture.
His admission works were *The Ray* and *The Buffet*, both now in the Louvre. Chardin was a prolific artist, producing
over a thousand paintings, but he never lost his fascination with familiar objects, which he rendered without artifice.
Quoting Chardin, Charles-Nicolas Cochin wrote: 'We use colours, but we paint with our feelings.'

JEAN HONORÉ FRAGONARD

The Bolt

Circa 1765 / Oil on canvas.

Fragonard loved to work in different genres and techniques. Instead of scattering his talent, his versatility seemed,
on the contrary, to stimulate him. Throughout his long career, which began under Louis XV and ended with
Napoleon, he favoured powerful, brilliant brush strokes. Writing of the daring subject treated in *The Bolt*,
the Goncourts declared: 'Impurity... knows no filth, nor disgust, nor shame.'
And they went on to add, 'The painting is a luminous inspiration.'

*'No matter how hard David tries, he is not
pompous. Pompous painters are born, not made...
Such softness, such surfaces! And never a dry spell.'*
Marc Chagall,
Les Dialogues du Louvre, *1991.*

JACQUES-LOUIS DAVID

The Lictors Bringing Brutus the Bodies of His Sons

1789 / Oil on canvas.

David's *Lictors* is an apologia for sacrifice and republican virtue –but it goes further. The painting is also an exploration
of the antagonism between the female universe and male inflexibility. Bright colours and fluid movements are used
to depict the female group, whose individual figures express several phases in an emotional outburst:
from the initial gesture of shock at the discovery of the dead figure to grief-stricken abandon.

THÉODORE GÉRICAULT

The Wounded Cuirassier

1814 / Oil on canvas.

Géricault exhibited at the Salon for the first time in 1812, at the age of 21. He died in 1824 after falling from a horse.
Those twelve short years encompass his career. Though he died too early to discover the exaltations of Romanticism,
his work is a masterly precursor.

*'One should not forget the enduring truth
of Delacroix's reflection: "First and foremost,
a figurative work should be a feast for the eyes".'*
André Masson, Le Plaisir de Peindre, *1950.*

EUGÈNE DELACROIX

Liberty Leading the People, 28 July 1830

1830 / Oil on canvas.

The ultimate Romantic, Delacroix expressed anger in the 1824 painting *Scenes of the Massacres of Scio, Greek Families Awaiting
Death or Slavery* and showed his enthusiasm for the Revolution of 1830 in *Liberty Leading the People*. In both paintings, the
artist, in a powerful burst of expressiveness, became a historical witness. In the 20th century, Picasso played a similar role when
he painted *Guernica*, in which he denounced the massacre committed during the Spanish Civil War.

*'Imagine an eye that would have stored all
the bodies encoutered in love, and that could
view them over and over again when
it set the stage of desire...'*
Bernard Noël,
Les Peintres du désir, *1992.*

JEAN AUGUSTE DOMINIQUE INGRES

The Turkish Bath

1862 / Oil on canvas, remounted on wood.
Painted when Ingres was 82, this composition is both a formal study of the nude and an example of the Orientalism then
in vogue. Previously owned by Prince Napoleon, the painting was acquired by the Société des Amis du Louvre in 1911.

*'Corot, the prophet
of gentle meditation
before the light, is not
exempt, when facing it,
of a pang of discreet
desolation...'*
André Masson,
Le Plaisir de Peindre,
1950.

JEAN-BAPTISTE
CAMILLE
COROT

**The Church
of Marissel,
near Beauvais**

1866 / Oil on canvas.

Beginning with Corot and
his close contemporaries,
the landscape was no
longer a simple back-
ground for archaeological
ruins or an accessory for
mythological scenes.
It was, in its own right,
the subject of the painting.
Corot's close attention
to the play of light and
his interest in landscape
make him a precursor of
the Impressionists.

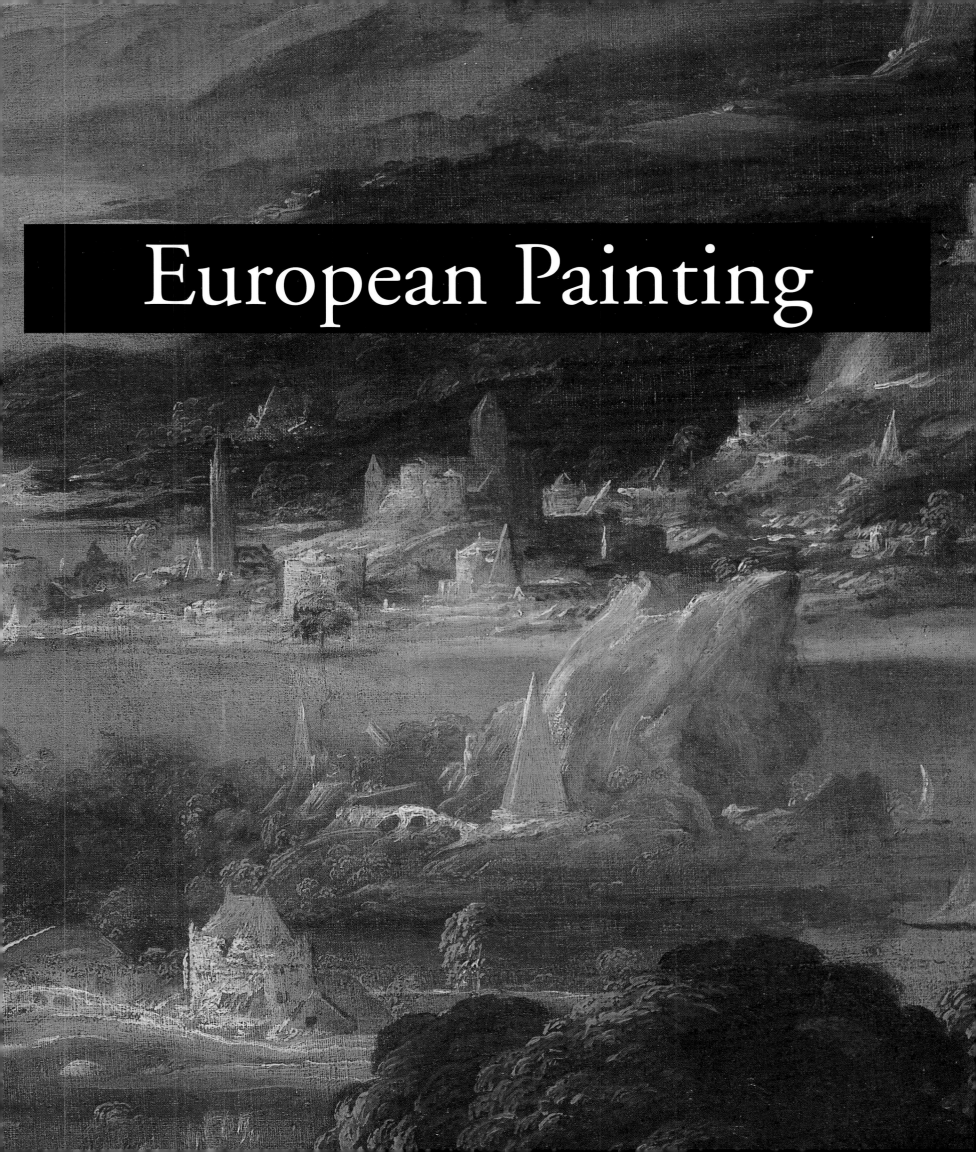

European Painting

Italian Painting. Spanish Painting. The Northern Schools of Painting.

The collections of European painting exhibited in the Richelieu and Denon wings of the Louvre are unrivalled, but the size of each of the national collections is not always representative of each country's significance in European art history.

The Italian collections

A fervent interest in Italian painting dominated French culture for several centuries, with the result that the Louvre has a large collection of Italian paintings, as is clearly illustrated by the inventories of Crown possessions that have been recorded since the Renaissance. Most of these works were assembled in the 17th century from collections such as those of Cardinal Mazarin and the banker Jabach. Many more works were later acquired through seizures during the revolutionary wars; others were looted during the Napoleonic campaigns –though many of these were returned after Napoleon's defeat, except for a few masterpieces like *The Marriage of Cana* by Veronese. In the 19th century, the Italian collections were enriched with some major acquisitions, including the large Campana collection, which revealed the early Italian masters to the general public.

Italy

From the early Italian masters to the Renaissance (late 13th-16th centuries). Italian painting may be said to begin with Cimabue–represented in the collections of the Louvre by *The Virgin and Child Enthroned and Surrounded by Angels,* a seminal work in the development of Western art. A generation later, Giotto developed Cimabue's innovations in frescoes and altarpieces –*Saint Francis of Assisi Receiving the Stigmata* is an example. The 15th century is represented by *The Coronation of the Virgin* by Fra Angelico, the master of the early Quattrocento, and by two exquisite portraits, one of *Ginevra d'Este* by Pisanello and the other of her husband and murderer, *Sigismondo Malatesta,* by Piero della Francesca.

Painted around 1455, *The Battle of San Romano* by Uccello is characteristic of Florentine artists' interest in perspective –be they sculptors, architects, or painters. The Louvre possesses several major paintings executed by members of the next generation. Among them are: Mantegna's *Saint Sebastian* and *A Young Woman Receives Presents from Venus and the Three Graces,* a fresco by Botticelli whose fluid lines and fresh colours create a poetic atmosphere that seems almost unreal. There are several masterpieces in the collections by Botticelli's contemporary Leonardo da Vinci, including *The Virgin of the Rocks, The Virgin and Child with Saint Anne,* and the portrait of a 24-year-old woman who

became famous as *Mona Lisa.* Other works from the golden age of Italian painting are Raphael's *Holy Family,* whose iconography was later copied all over Europe, and his portrait of *Baldassare Castiglione,* who sits in a pose that is reminiscent of that of the *Mona Lisa.* During this time, Florence ceased being the only major art centre in Italy. North of Florence was Parma, where Correggio worked his voluptuously thick brush strokes. Farther north lay Venice, the city whose artists would dominate the 16th century with their vibrant brush strokes and golden hues, as illustrated by Tintoretto's *Sketch for 'Paradise',* Titian's *Pastoral Concert* and Veronese's *Marriage at Cana.*

Neoclassical and Baroque art (late 16th-17th centuries). Two major innovators emerge at the end of the 16th century: Annibale Carracci, the father of the school of Bologna, and Caravaggio, who is represented at the Louvre by *The Death of the Virgin,* one of his most poignantly moving canvases. The artists, who both worked in Rome, greatly influenced 16th-century Italian art, especially such painters as Guercino, Guido Reni, and Domenichino –whose *Landscape with the Flight into Egypt* is an excellent illustration of Carracci's influence– as well as artists all over Europe. Although there are some major gaps in the Louvre's 18th-century collections of Italian art, the museum nonetheless possesses some powerful works, including a *Last Supper* by Giovanni Battista Tiepolo, a *Carnival Scene* by his son Domenico, a series of scenes of Venetian festivals by Guardi, and several works by Pannini, whose influence on the French artist Hubert Robert is apparent.

Spain

Spanish painting was long neglected by French collectors, with the result that it is poorly represented at the Louvre. In the 19th century, however, a collection of Spanish art was assembled for Louis-Philippe by Baron Taylor. When five rooms dedicated to Spanish art were finally inaugurated at the Louvre in 1838, the collection comprised about 600 works, including eight paintings by El Greco, 19 by Velázquez, 60 by Zurbarán, 38 by Murillo, and 8 by Goya. After the Revolution of 1848, the collection was returned to the family of the Duc d'Orléans, who sold it through Christie's in 1853.

The Louvre has some works by 15th-century Catalan masters, such as *The Flagellation of Saint George* by Bernardo Martorell and *The Flagellation of Christ,* from the Cathedral of Barcelona, by Jaime Huguet. The 16th century is exemplified by El Greco's *Christ on the Cross Adored by Two Donors,* painted when the artist was at the summit of his talent. The following century is represented by Ribera's famous *Beggar,* also known as *The Club-foot,* and Murillo's

Preceding pages

NICOLO DELL'ABATE

The Rape of Persephone

Circa 1560 / Oil on canvas (detail).

Nicolo dell'Abate, a renowned fresco artist from Bologna, was invited to work in France by Henri II. While there, he executed numerous decorations, most notably the ballroom at Fontainebleau, conceived under the direction of Primaticcio. *The Rape of Persephone* is an excellent example of the artist's work, revealing him as a great colourist endowed with a visionary imagination.

Young Beggar; the harsh realism of both paintings offers a severe criticism of their society. Also dating from the 17th century are several magnificent works by Zurbarán, such as *The Lying-in-State of Saint Bonaventure* and *Saint Apollonia.* Goya towers over the 18th century with a number of excellent portraits, including that of *The Countess of Carpio, Marquesa de la Solana,* painted around 1793. The sombre grey and black tones, heightened by a splash of pink, seem to emphasise the psychological gravity of the model as she hovers between gentle fragility and sadness.

Great Britain

Long indifferent to British painting, the curators of the Louvre did not begin collecting works by British artists until the late 19th century. With the notable exception of the portrait of *Edward VI* by William Scrots, dated 1550, the collections at the Louvre begin with some major 18th-century portraits, including *Master Hare* by Reynolds, Gainsborough's *Conversation in a Park* and his magnificent *Lady Alston,* which, despite its elegant classicism, is laden with mysterious Romantic charm. An air of Romanticism also envelopes *Lady Macbeth* by Fuseli, the Anglo-Swiss illustrator of Shakespeare. The early 19th century is represented by a *View of Salisbury* by Constable, who influenced many artists across the Channel, most notably Delacroix. With the acquisition of Turner's *Landscape with Distant River and Bay,* the Louvre added to its collections a work that is on the threshold of abstraction.

Germanic countries

Although the Louvre's collection of paintings from the Germanic countries is small, it is of excellent quality. It includes some remarkable works by 15th-century masters such as *The Altarpiece of the Seven Joys of Mary,* executed around 1480 by the Master of the Holy Kindred of the school of Cologne. The better-known Renaissance artists include Dürer, whose famous *Portrait of the Artist Holding an Erynganeum,* executed in 1493, is the painter's only work in a French collection. Another artist of the same generation is Lucas Cranach the Elder, exemplified by *Venus Standing in a Landscape.* Works from the first half of the 16th century include *The Knight, the Young Girl, and Death* by Hans Baldung Grien and several portraits by Hans Holbein, which were originally part of Louis XIV's collections. They include portraits of *Erasmus,* author of *The Praise of Folly,* and the astronomer *Nicholas Kratzer.* Works from subsequent centuries are minor, with the exception of *Tree with Crows,* the uncontested manifesto of Romanticism, painted in 1822 by Caspar David Friedrich, one of the most significant painters of the early 19th century.

Flanders and Holland

The Louvre's Flemish and Dutch collections, containing over 1,000 paintings, date back to the 17th century. The paintings, including the monumental series painted by Rubens for Marie de' Medici and numerous works by Van Dyck, exercised a strong influence on French painting. The early royal collection was enlarged in the 17th century by D'Angiviller's ambitious policy of acquisitions. Although some significant purchases were made in the 19th century, a more important role was played by donations like the La Caze bequest, which included works by Frans Hals, Rubens, Rembrandt, and Teniers.

Fifteenth- and sixteenth-century Flemish and Dutch art is illustrated by several masterpieces, including *The Annunciation* by Van der Weyden, painted around 1435, and Van Eyck's *Virgin of Chancellor Rolin,* in which the minutely rendered detail has a spiritual and poetic dimension. The Louvre also possesses several works by Memling, including *The Triptych of the Resurrection, with the Martyrdom of Saint Sebastian and the Ascension. The Ship of Fools* by Hieronymus Bosch and *The Moneylender and his Wife* by Quentin Metsys both date from the turn of the century. The collections are well endowed with exceptional works from the 16th century, exemplified by *The Lamentation of Christ* by Joos van Cleve and *The Beggars* by Pieter Brueghel the Elder.

In the 16th century, the golden age of Flemish painting, its influence spread all over Europe, especially to France. Works by painters active at the beginning of the century include a *Stag Hunt* by Paul Bril and the fabulous *Battle of Issus* by Jan Brueghel, known as Velvet Brueghel, which was presented to Louis XIV by Le Nôtre. Other major works include *Helena Fourment with a Carriage* by Rubens; a fine portrait of the ill-fated *Charles I, King of England, Hunting* by Van Dyck; the beautifully constructed *Jesus Driving the Merchants from the Temple* by Jordaens; and Teniers' *Heron Hunt,* in which the artist demonstrates that his talent goes beyond the depiction of tavern scenes.

Seventeenth-century Dutch art is also well represented by such works as Gerrit van Honthorst's *Concert* and by Frans Hal's *Gypsy Girl.* The Louvre possesses numerous works by Rembrandt: *Bathsheba at her Bath,* so magnificently drenched in golden light, and many self-portraits that express a variety of moods –from swaggering and joking to pained and worried. The 17th century is also the period of Ruysdael (known for his marvelous skies), Metsu, Ter Borch, Pieter de Hooch, and Vermeer, whose *Lacemaker* gives the viewer a glimpse of a secret world suspended in the infinite silence of the canvas.

Italian painting

From Cimabue to Caravaggio

AT THE DAWN OF THE 14TH CENTURY, Dante's traveller, lost in the 'dark forest', saw the light of day, and Cimabue passed away. The two –writer and painter– were the harbingers of the Renaissance. Italy, then dominated by prosperous cities ruled by powerful banking and merchant families, developed an extensive system of art patronage that would result in an unparalleled flowering of the arts. In Florence, the artists under the patronage and protection of Cosimo de' Medici included the architect Brunelleschi, the sculptor Donatello, and the painter Fra Angelico. And it was in Florence that Cimabue, the first artist to break with Byzantine art, became the first truly Italian painter; later, Giotto, who was probably his student, made the transition from an art form that was still medieval to the new humanist age. The Quattrocento saw the rise of such diverse artists as Uccello, Masaccio, Mantegna, Piero della Francesca, and Botticelli.

ITALIAN RENAISSANCE ART REACHED A PEAK of innovation between the late 15th and the mid-16th centuries: Leonardo da Vinci developed his famous *sfumato,* a technique that gave forms a slightly hazy quality; the tormented genius of Michelangelo created powerful forms that were the precursors of Baroque art; and Raphael, with his excellent draughtsmanship and use of colour, created a subtle alchemy that would exemplify Classicism.

THE 16TH CENTURY SAW THE TRIUMPH of the Venetian school. Its artists developed a highly elegant style with rich warm colours bathed in a characteristic bronze-tinted light. From Giorgone to Titian, from Tintoretto to Veronese, the artists of the Venetian school are universally appealing, whether in large monumental mural pieces or smaller easel paintings. The charm and refinement of their style are exemplified by Titian's *Pastoral Concert* and Veronese's *Marriage at Cana.*

FOLLOWING THE DEATH OF THE GREAT VENETIAN MASTERS, Bologna replaced Venice as Italy's artistic centre. The Carracci family developed a new, simpler style in reaction to the excessive virtuosity of Mannerism. Meanwhile, in Rome, Caravaggio was developing a naturalistic style in which light played a highly innovative, expressive role. The influence of these artists on later European art was immense, but would, paradoxically, signal the end of Italian artistic supremacy. The brilliance of some of Venice's great 18th-century artists, such as Guardi and Canaletto, did not suffice to revive Italy's past artistic grandeur.

CENNI DI PEPO, known as CIMABUE

The Virgin and Child Enthroned and Surrounded by Angels

Circa 1270 / Paint on wood.

'It's the most beautiful painting in the Louvre. It is serenity itself: everything is practically on the same level, but the golden heavens create a strange perspective, with different planes. It makes me think of ancient Chinese landscapes, in which walls of fog separate the planes. Such an amazing composition: in the outline of the wings and of the throne, and in the shape of the frame! The gold creates holes in the painting, but they let the painting breathe. They are like springs at the bottom of a lake!' Zao Wou-ki, *Les Dialogues du Louvre*, 1991.

*'It is one of the greatest masterpieces of the Louvre
because of its great rigour: lances, agitated legs,
repetitions, a verticality that is constantly
broken by oblique lines, and spaces created
by movements that are apparently uniform
—the whole lightened by a few decorative curves
(the banners).'*
Pierre Soulages,
Les Dialogues du Louvre, *1991.*

PAOLO DI DONO, known as UCCELLO

The Battle of San Romano

*Circ*a 1455 / Paint on wood.

To illustrate the Florentine victory over Siena at the Battle of San Romano in 1432, Uccello painted three large scenes.
The left-hand side, now at the National Gallery in London, shows the Florentine commander Niccolò da Tolentino.
In the middle scene, now at the Uffizi Gallery in Florence, the Sienese commander Bernardino della Ciarda
is unhorsed. This panel, which hung on the right, shows the counterattack led by Micheletto da Cotignola
that secured the Florentine victory.

*'Leonardo da Vinci,
deep dark mirror,
Where charming angels
with sweet smiles
Laden with mystery,
appear in the shadows
Of glaciers
and pine trees that
enclose their country.'*
Charles Baudelaire,
Les Fleurs du Mal,
1857.

LEONARDO
DI SER PIERO
DA VINCI,
known as
LEONARDO
DA VINCI

The Mona Lisa,
also known as
La Gioconda

1503-1506
Oil on wood.

Arguably the most famous
painting in the world,
The Mona Lisa is the
portrait of the young wife
of a Florentine dignitary,
Francesco Bartolomeo
di Zanoli del Giocondo.
Leonardo took the
painting with him to
France and kept it
throughout his life.
It was later purchased
by François I.

RAFFAELLO SANZIO, known as RAPHAEL

Baldassare Castiglione

Circa 1514-1515 / Oil on canvas.

A friend of Raphael's, Baldassare Castiglione, diplomat and author of *The Book of the Courtier*, looks amiably
out of the canvas, seeming to meet the artist's gaze. The work may also be seen as a tribute to Leonardo da Vinci
(and to *The Mona Lisa*, whose pose is similar), who greatly influenced the young Raphael.

TIZIANO VECELLIO known as TITIAN

The Pastoral Concert

Circa 1510-1511 / Oil on canvas.

Now attributed to Titian, *The Pastoral Concert* was until recently thought to have been executed by Giorgione.
The scene it represents, the happy, peaceful Arcadia of Greek mythology, was a favourite subject of Renaissance artists.
When it appeared again in the 17th century, notably in the work of Nicolas Poussin,
the interpretation was more cynical.

*'We can take in the whole painting, or simply visit
it one detail at a time. The artist has
simultaneously mastered both approaches.'
Pierre Soulages,*
Dialogues du Louvre, *1991.*

PAOLO CALIARI, known as VERONESE

The Marriage at Cana

1562-1563 / Oil on canvas.

This immense canvas was painted for the refectory of the Benedictine convent in San Giorgio Maggiore, in Venice.
Legend has it that artists of the period are portrayed among the musicians: Veronese himself is the musician dressed in
white; facing him is Titian, dressed in red and playing the bass viol; between them sit Bassano, blowing into a cornet,
and Tintoretto, playing the violin. According to tradition, several princes of the period are depicted among
the wedding guests, including François I, the Holy Roman Emperor Charles V, and Süleyman the Magnificent.
The painting was seized by Napoleon's troops during the Italian campaign and entered the Louvre in 1798.
It is one of the few paintings not returned after the defeat of the Empire.

'It was painted for the Church of Santa Maria della Scala in Trastevere, but despite the regard in which the painter was held, this work was rejected.
The Virgin's body, lying with such little decorum, resembles the corpse of a drowned woman and seems scarcely noble enough to represent the Mother of God. It was removed from the church, and having been purchased by the Duke of Mantua, was sent to England, from where it was brought here.'
André Félibien,
Entretiens sur les vies et les ouvrages des plus excellents peintres...,
1679.

MICHELANGELO
MERISI,
known as
CARAVAGGIO

**The Death
of the Virgin**

1605-1606

At the turn of the 16th century, European painting was strongly influenced by Caravaggio's powerful realism and the violent contrasts of his chiaroscuro. He often found his models in Rome's poor quarters, where he worked. The model for the figure of the Virgin was a prostitute. Caravaggio was forced to leave Rome suddenly in 1606, following a fight in which he mortally wounded his opponent. He never returned.

Spanish Painting

From El Greco to Goya

AT THE BEGINNING OF THE 8TH CENTURY, the Moors imposed their rule and culture on most of the Iberian Peninsula. Although a few minor kingdoms in the north resisted, the Christians did not regain complete control of Spain until the end of the 15th century, when the country was unified under the Catholic Queen Isabella.

DURING THE 15TH CENTURY, artists like Bernardo Martorell and Jaime Huguet developed their own distinctive styles, which were nevertheless steeped in International Gothic. Frequent contacts with French, Italian, and Flemish artists left their mark on Spanish painting: Bartolomé Bermejo, who was born in Cordoba, learned his craft in Flanders and made an extended visit to Naples, while the Castilian artist Pedro Berruguete spent several years in Italy, where he probably met Piero della Francesca.

DURING THE FOLLOWING CENTURY, Spain entered a period of economic prosperity and independence, but in the domain of the arts it remained under the sway of the great movements stirring Renaissance Europe. Fernández Navarrete, who was born around 1526, made an extensive tour of Italy, visiting Rome, Florence, Naples, and Venice. The work of his contemporary Sánchez Coello reveals a strong affinity with Titian and Correggio. But the Golden Age of Spanish painting is dominated by the genius of El Greco, who moved in 1577 to Toledo, where he developed his exaltedly mystical style.

ALTHOUGH EL GRECO had his followers during the early years of the 17th century, a fascination soon developed with Caravaggio and the school of Bologna. The association of influences favoured the development of a genuine Spanish school in the 17th century, exemplified by Zurbarán, known for his sombre Tenebrism and exquisite palette; Ribera, with his monumental figures and powerful naturalism; and Velázquez, 'the painter's painter', as Manet described him.

EIGHTEENTH-CENTURY Spanish painters, like artists throughout the rest of Europe, developed a light, airy Baroque style (the Tiepolos worked in Madrid during the 1760's), before seeking more rigorous forms of expression. Goya's genius stands out among the painters of this period. 'He does not herald one of the artists of our time: he prefigures all of modern art, because modern art begins with that very freedom.'

DOMENICOS THEOTOCOPOULOS, known as EL GRECO

Christ on the Cross, worshipped by two donors

Circa 1585-1590 / Oil on canvas.

Picasso said: 'I had seen some of his paintings and had been greatly moved by them...
It is probably due to his influence that I painted elongated figures during my Blue Period.'
Brassaï, *Conversations avec Picasso* (16 June 1944), 1964.

'I too loved Veronese and Zurbarán, but it is the 17th century that spells perfection.'
Paul Cézanne,
Ambroise Vollard,
Conversations avec
Cézanne, *1978.*

FRANCISCO DE ZURBARÁN

Saint Apollonia

Circa 1635-1640 /
Oil on canvas.

The saint can be recognised by her one of her attributes: a tooth held up with a set of pincers, symbolising her martyrdom, during which her torturers struck her on the jaw and made her teeth fall out. This painting belongs to the artist's more prolific period. Though a highly mystical painter, Zurbarán did not let his spirituality stop him from experimenting with a brightly coloured palette in which luminous folds of drapery play a major part.

FRANCISCO
JOSÉ DE GOYA
Y LUCIENTES

**The Countess
of Carpio,
Marquesa
de la Solana**

Circa 1794 /
Oil on canvas.

Goya became deaf
following an attack
of cerebral meningitis in
1793, which had also left
him temporarily paralysed.
When he recovered
sufficiently to work again,
he painted this portrait
of the Marquesa de la
Solana, who appears
both gentle and sad.
The Marquesa, then aged
37, knew she was ill and
did not have long to live;
she commissioned
this portrait as a
remembrance
for her daughter.

Painting of the Northern schools

From Jan Van Eyck to Caspar David Friedrich

IN THE LATE 14TH CENTURY, International Gothic spread all over Europe. It was a brilliantly appealing style, though at times overly precious. In the 1430's, artists such as Konrad Witz in Germany, and Jan Van Eyck and Van der Weyden in the Low Countries developed a more realistic style favouring minutely rendered detail and a sharp sense of light and space. The Flemish influence was dominant among the following generation, which included such dissimilar artists as Memling and Bosch.

AT THE END OF THE 15TH CENTUY and the beginning of the following century, Northern Europe discovered Italian art. A new Renaissance style emerged from the meeting of the Italian style with Flemish naturalism and local traditions. In Germany, artists working in the new style included Dürer, Cranach, and Holbein the Younger; in the Low Countries, they included Metsys and Lucas van Leiden. In Northern Europe at this time there were many important art centres, each working in its own style; some artists sought a serene expression of reality and others an exuberant Mannerism. And in this tangle of Italian and Northern influences (which also included Vienna and Prague) some great artists remained outside the main-stream: Pieter Brueghel, for example, followed a variety of directions, including those established by the landscape art of the Flemish painter Patinir and the moralising verve of the Dutch artist Hieronymus Bosch.

IN THE 16TH CENTURY, several foreign styles —notably Caravaggism— made their way to Northern Europe, where they sometimes, as in Germany, neutralised the development of distinctive local styles. Some artists towered over their peers. Among the Flemish artists, Rubens successfully blended the modern Italian style with national traditions; until the 19th century, his style and palette would be adopted by artists all over Europe. Van Dyck inspired numerous French artists, although his influence would primarily make itself felt in 18th-century Britain through Reynolds and Gainsborough. In Holland, several great talents emerged: Frans Hals, the portrait painter; Ruysdael, the landscape artist; and, above all, Vermeer, the poet of silent inner life, and Rembrandt, who, dissatisfied with simply representing reality, would transfigure it.

AFTER THE FINAL BURST OF RENAISSANCE GLORY, it was not till the emergence of Romanticism that Northern Europe nurtured another generation of profoundly original talents, including the Anglo-Swiss painter Johann Henrich Fuseli and the German artist Caspar David Friedrich.

JAN VAN EYCK

The Virgin of Chancellor Rolin

Circa 1435 / Oil on wood.

A high dignitary of the Burgundy Court, Chancellor Nicolas Rolin commissioned this deeply religious work for his chapel in the Church of Notre-Dame in Autun. He is shown praying before a Virgin and child. The city depicted in the background in minutely rendered detail is not real, though some parts of it have been identified as Liege. Jan Van Eyck was the Valet of the Bedchamber of the Duke of Burgundy, Philippe the Good, in whose service he remained until he died in 1441.

PIETER BRUEGHEL THE ELDER

The Beggars

1568 / Paint on wood.

The inscription on the back of the painting, 'Legless cripple, cheer up, and may you prosper', is as fierce
as the monstrous ballet shown on the canvas. The burlesque parade of beggars threateningly armed with crutches
and wearing bizarre hats and tunics with fox-tails attached may be interpreted as a frighteningly derisive
depiction of human suffering.

*'Rubens, such a generous painter!
We feel it doesn't bother him to squeeze a hundred figures onto a canvas!
There's someone who doesn't worry about counting cheeks…'
Auguste Renoir.*

PETER PAUL
RUBENS

**The Landing
of Marie de' Medici
at Marseilles**

Circa 1622-1625
Oil on canvas.

Rubens executed a series of twenty-four monumental paintings in lavish colours on the life of Marie de' Medici for her residence at the Luxembourg Palace. Commissioned by Marie de' Medici herself, the immense decorative cycle is an epic account of the political events that marked her life.
An exceptional artist, Rubens was renowned all over Europe.
True to his friendship with Marie de' Medici, he later gave her sanctuary in his house in Cologne when she was exiled by her son Louis XIII.

REMBRANDT HARMENSZ VAN RIJN

Bathsheba at her Bath

1654 / Oil on canvas.

The episode of Bathsheba being surprised in her bath by King David had been frequently depicted by artists, but Rembrandt chose to treat the subject in a different manner. The king does not appear in the painting and is simply evoked by the letter held in Bathsheba's hand. This is one of the most beautiful nude paintings of the century. The model is probably Hendrickje Stoffels, Rembrandt's mistress.

JOHANNES VERMEER

The Lacemaker

Circa 1670-1671 / Canvas on wood.

Vermeer's Delft had a lively artistic scene, but he set himself apart by breaking with genre painting
to focus on the representation of the subtle emotions of silent inner life.

CASPAR DAVID FRIEDRICH

The Tree with Crows

Circa 1822 / Oil on canvas.

In a letter to Heinrich Meyer, Goethe wrote: 'Enclosed please find, dear friend, art works by Friedrich, well protected and sealed, as they came to me. My sole regret is that we have not been able to look at them together; perfection is so rare! To such an extent that one must appreciate it and take pleasure in it even when it presents itself under a strange light...'

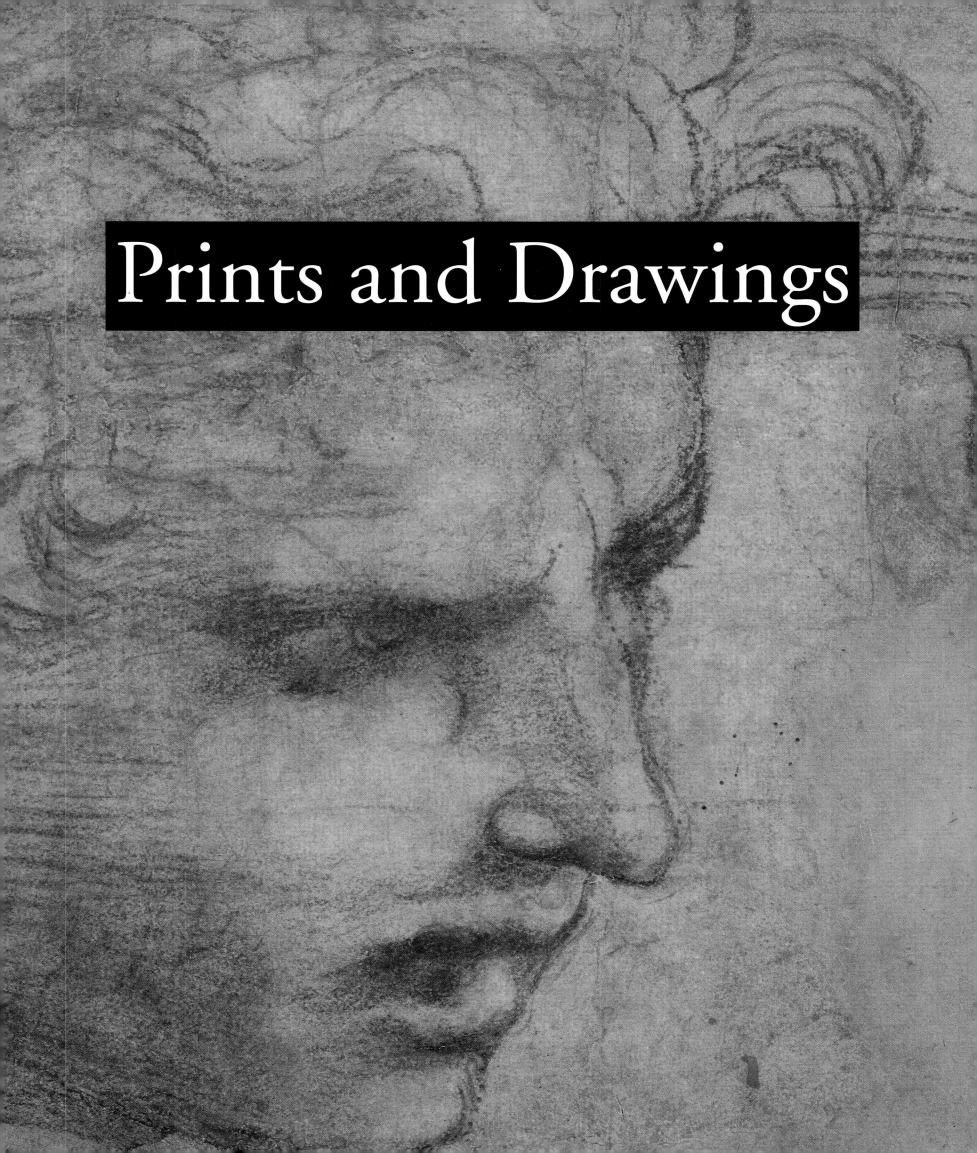

Prints and Drawings

Prints and Drawings

The Department of Prints and Drawings is located in the Pavillon de Flore, the only vestige, apart from the Pavillon de Marsan, of the Tuileries Palace. The Louvre's collection of prints and drawings is one of the most renowned in the world, along with the Albertina's in Vienna. The collection contains more than 150,000 works, partly obtained through purchases and partly through the acquisition of the ateliers of early official royal painters (Le Brun, Mignard, Coypel). Other works, including those in the Saint-Morys collection, were requisitioned from emigrants during the Revolution. Additional works were acquired through bequests and donations, including those of His de la Salle and Gatteaux in the 19th century, and Léon Bonnat and Étienne Moreau-Nélaton in the 20th century. The Edmond de Rothschild collection, donated in 1936, constitutes a separate, independent Room of Drawings with approximately 40,000 prints, 3,000 drawings, and 500 illustrated books.

The Department of Prints and Drawings includes a section on Chalcography containing roughly 16,000 original copperplates dating from the Renaissance to the present. They are still used to make prints that are sold through the outlets of the Réunion des Musées Nationaux.

The French school abounds in graphic works produced in a variety of techniques, ranging from the *Narbonne Altar Frontal*, a black-ink monochrome on silk, dated *circa* 1375, produced by a Paris atelier, to *David Sparing Saul,* an exquisite Renaissance drawing in pierre noire with a brown wash and white highlights, by Antoine Caron. The great collections begin in the 17th century with some magnificent works by Nicolas Poussin, including the pen-and-wash *Venus at the Fountain,* and Simone Vouet's touching *Portrait of a Little Girl* (one of 250 drawings by the artist). In addition, there are works by Le Lorrain (e.g., the peaceful *Shepherd on the Banks of a Lake),* Champaigne, Le Brun, La Hyre, Le Sueur, and Sébastien Bourdon. The 18th century is represented by some remarkable works by Watteau, including a *Female Nude* in red chalk and pierre noire, whose face the artist has hidden —as he so often did in his works, and by Chardin's famous pastel *Self-Portrait at the Easel.* Edme Bouchardon, regarded as the greatest draughtsman of his time, has left some excellent works, including *Nymph in her Bath with Shepherds,* in red chalk. The 19th century is represented by several works by David, most notably the preparatory sketches for *Consecration of the Emperor Napoleon I.* Although the collection of drawings by Ingres is much smaller than the one at Montauban, it nonetheless possesses some excellent works, such as the preparatory sketch for the *Portrait of Madame Marcotte de Sainte-Marie,* which is also at the Louvre. Prud'hon's *Female Academy,* in black-and-white pencil on fine blue paper,

portrays a feeling of great sensuality. There is also a major collection of powerful works in lead pencil and watercolour by Delacroix, including his wonderful *Moroccan Notebook.*

The Italian school shows off its riches in the collections. Among works from the 15th century are Verrocchio's *Female Head with Downcast Eyes,* in metal point, grey wash, and white gouache on prepared orange-pink paper; and an excellent ink drawing by Jacopo Bellini for *The Funeral of the Virgin.* The 16th century is represented by Leonardo da Vinci's exquisite studies of *Draperies of Seated Figures,* in pierre noire and ink wash with white highlights, Raphael's *Head of a Young Man in Three-Quarters Profile,* Michelangelo's *Nude Studies,* and Parmesan's gently Mannerist *Two Vase Carriers,* in red chalk and brown ink with white highlights. Other 17th-century artists deserving mention include Veronese, the Bassanos, and Castiglione (represented by *The Holy Family Returning from Egypt).* There are also some excellent 18th-century works, including Giambattista Tiepolo's *Statue* and Piranesi's *Palace Interior.*

The Northern schools are very well represented, with some understandably biased examples, such as Maertens van Heemskerck's *Roman Coliseum,* an ink drawing dated 1570, and Lucas van Leiden's handsome *Portrait of a Man.* Seventeenth-century works include a watercolour-and-gouache *Coronation of the Virgin* by Jacob Jordaens, some excellent wash drawings by Rembrandt, and *Kneeling Woman,* executed with great virtuosity in pierre noire and red chalk with white highlights by Rubens. Germany is represented by the famous *View of Val d'Arco,* executed in watercolour and gouache by Dürer during a trip to Italy; an unusual drawing in pierre noire by Matthias Grünewald depicting a *Smiling Old Woman;* and Friedrich's *Cemetery under the Moon,* executed in wash around 1835 and given by the artist to the sculptor David d'Angers. Great Britain is represented by some excellent works, including several drawings by Gainsborough, a lovely *View of the Château of Saint-Germain-en-Laye* by Turner, and *Satan and Beelzebub,* an astonishing work in pierre noire with white highlights by Thomas Lawrence, which is characteristic of the works of English artists like John Martin and William Blake, who at the end of the rationalist 18th century brought a welcome breath of visionary Romanticism.

Preceding pages

RAFFAELLO
SANZIO,
known as
RAPHAEL

**Head
of a Young Man
in Three-Quarters
Profile, Facing Right**

Rome 1511-1514
Pierre noire, charcoal,
red wash, with grey wash
and white highlights,
on grey-beige paper, traces
of squaring in pierre noire
(detail).

Drawing for the fresco
of *Heliodorus Driven from
the Temple* in the papal
apartments of the Vatican.

Looking at a drawing....

'DRAWING IS THE MELODY, and colour the harmony,' said Théophile Gautier. The drawing is what disappears under a covering of paint; it is the absence that gives shape and serves as the 'scaffolding' of a visual representation.

EVEN BEFORE IS COPIED onto a canvas, where it acts as a skeleton, a rough sketch on a piece of paper may also serve in helping to structure the composition of a painting or to study an anatomical detail. Yet viewed on its own, a drawing may seem austere. The power of drawing as an art form resides in the limited means that it grants itself. In examining a drawing, the viewer seeks a feeling of immediacy with the creative process, as well as that sense of spontaneity inherent in each stroke or gesture, on which there is no going back.

SOME DRAWINGS may be likened to the playing of scales, a repetition that can help solve a specific problem, such as depicting the reflection of a light source, or making an ascending form appear lighter. This is what we see in the 3,000 works by Le Brun –for the most part found at his home after his death–and in the 2,000 works by Eugène Delacroix.

SOME EXCEPTIONAL DRAWINGS may aspire to the status of finished works. Drawings executed in pierre noire by Michelangelo and washes by Poussin are good examples. For some artists, drawing is an art form in its own right, but whatever the goal of a drawing, it is defined by several aspects: the nature of the support and its quality, colour, and porosity; the technique, whether metal point, goose quill, metal nib, or brush; the various pigments that were favoured during different periods –pierre noire in the 16th century, brown wash (often black ink that has faded over the years) in the 17th century, red chalk and pastel in the 18th century, and watercolour in the 19th century. Nonetheless, when Dürer worked in metal point, Corot in lead pencil, Watteau in 'three crayons', and Chardin in pastels, their choices were not entirely governed by passing fashions but reflected more profound changes in the history of taste.

IS DRAWING AN AUSTERE ART FORM? An aura of elitism seems to have attached itself to the appreciation of the graphic arts. The great collectors of prints and drawings whose names have been recorded –Vasari during the Renaissance, Queen Christina of Sweden and Jabach in the 17th century, Mariette and the Duke of Devonshire in the 18th century– were all regarded as great connoisseurs. As Diderot wrote, 'The "half-connoisseur" will walk past a drawing masterpiece without stopping'. It is true that he art of drawing deserves ample time for study.

MICHELANGELO BUONARROTI, known as MICHELANGELO

Standing Male Nude

Rome or Florence, early 16th century / Pen and brown ink.

ALBRECHT DÜRER

View of Val d'Arco

1495 / Watercolour and gouache, retouched with pen and black ink.

Like so many Northern European artists, Dürer travelled to Italy. While there in 1494 and 1495, he executed about fifteen
watercolour landscapes, including the *View of Val d'Arco* reproduced here, regarded as the absolute masterpiece of the series.

NICOLAS POUSSIN

Venus at the Fountain

17 August 1657 / Pen and brown ink, brown and grey wash.

Poussin was as great a graphic artist as he was a painter, as attested by the quality of the work reproduced here. Venus's arms are shown in alternative positions, so that she seems to have three. Three-armed figures can also be seen in the preparatory sketches for Ingres' *Turkish Bath* and Rembrandt's engraving *The French-style Bed*.

CHARLES LE BRUN

The Nations of Asia: Cartoon for the Ambassadors' Stairs

Paris, 1674-1677 / Pierre noire and white chalk, with red chalk highlights, on beige paper mounted on canvas.

Sketches for the decoration of the Ambassadors' Stairs at the Château de Versailles,
executed by Lebrun between 1676 and 1679.
The monumental stairway was destroyed by Louis XV to make room for the royal opera.

JEAN SIMÉON CHARDIN

Self-Portrait at the Easel

1771 / Pastel on blue paper over a canvas stretcher.

Chardin used pastels, a very popular form in the 18th century, to portray himself and his wife.
The portraits, which date from the end of his life, reveal a profound psychological introspection,
hitherto unknown in his work.

Decorative Arts

Decorative Arts

Preceding pages

THE GALERIE D'APOLLON

In 1663, Charles Le Brun was commissioned to decorate the gallery. To glorify Louis XIV, he chose the subject of Apollo for the mural decorations, but he completed only two paintings, *The Triumph of the Waters* and *Diana, or Night.* From 1850 to 1851, Eugène Delacroix executed the central ceiling painting, *Apollo Defeating the Serpent Python.*

The Department of Decorative Arts possesses thousands of works from many countries, spanning the periods from the High Middle Ages to the Second Empire. They come from many different sources, including the early royal collections–assembled for the most part by Louis XIV and later kings–and part of the treasure of the Abbey of Saint-Denis, which entered the Louvre in 1793. The collections were further enriched in the 19th and 20th centuries through purchases and donations; additional works were directly transferred from the *Mobilier National.*

The Middle Ages (3rd-15th centuries). From this vast period, a number of landmark pieces pinpoint stylistic developments and the use of varied materials, from the Graeco-Roman tradition of the Late Empire, Byzantine art, Carolingian and 11th-century Romanesque art, up to the apotheosis of Flamboyant Gothic, which preceded the Renaissance. Some major early works include *The Emperor Triumphant* (also known as *The Barberini Ivory),* a magnificent 6th-century relief from Constantinople, in which Christ is shown blessing the Emperor Justinian; and a Carolingian bronze, *Equestrian Statuette of Charlemagne,* probably cast in Aix-la-Chapelle in the 9th century. Works that had been stored in the treasury of the Abbey of Saint-Denis include the *Coronation Sword of the Kings of France* (9th-10th centuries) and an eagle-shaped porphyry vase with a gilded silver and niello inlay, known as *Suger's Eagle (circa* 1140). From the Gothic period, there is a *Virgin and Child,* presented to the Abbey of Saint-Denis by Queen Jeanne d'Évreux, that is richly decorated in silver gilt, with translucent enamels, rock crystal, precious stones, and pearls. *The Sceptre of Charles V* dates from the late 14th century. Jean Fouquet's 15th-century *Self-Portrait* is regarded as the first self-portrait in French art history.

The Renaissance (15th-16th centuries) is represented by many remarkable pieces. Since they cannot all be mentioned, the following Italian bronzes are cited as examples: *Saint Jerome and the Lion* (late 15th century) by Bellano, who studied with Donatello, and works by Jean de Boulogne (Giambologna) such as *Nessus and Deianira* (16th century). From 16th-century France, there are several enamels by Léonard Limosin, including the *Portrait of the Connétable de Montmorency,* numerous glazed clays by Bernard Palissy, and several exquisite tapestries, including *Maximilian's Hunt,* woven in Brussels around 1530 after a cartoon by the Flemish painter Van Orley.

From the 17th century, we have inherited many tapestries. Among the most beautiful are those designed by Simon de Vouet –some of which were woven in the workshops set up in the Grande Galerie of the Louvre before the creation of the Gobelins factory in 1662. Works in ceramics include several pieces from Nevers, attesting to the excellent quality of the work produced there. The furniture in the collections shows numerous developments in interior decoration, from the style of the Renaissance, which was still popular under Louis XIII, to the luxurious marquetry pieces produced by Boulle in his workshops in the Louvre from 1672 till his death in 1732.

From the 18th century are several fine pieces by Charles Cressent and Matthieu Criaerd, who worked under Louis XV, and by Martin Carlin and Jean-Henri Riesener, working under Louis XVI. They show that once a style emerges, it is rapidly adopted regardless of the manner in which it is produced –whether by artists working on unique pieces or by craftsmen. There are some exquisite examples of gold and silverware, including the silver *Centrepiece* belonging to Joseph I of Portugal, designed by Germain, and the *Wine Cooler,* designed by Edme-Pierre Balzac. Mention should also be made of Madame de Pompadour's collection of Sèvres porcelain.

The First Empire emphasised the Neoclassical rigour that had become popular at the end of the 18th century. The most characteristic example is the furniture produced by the cabinetmaker Jacob-Desmalter, who designed the desk of the president of the French National Assembly. The Louvre has in its collections the *Jewel Cabinet* that he produced for the Empress Joséphine, following the architect Percier's design. After the Empire, the fashion was for more elaborately ornate styles; the reign of Louis-Philippe saw the emergence of several revival styles: neo-Gothic, neo-Renaissance, and neo-Rococo. It also popularised exoticism, as illustrated by Queen Marie-Amélie's *Chinese Breakfast Set.* The Second Empire further developed a taste for the lavish, with gold-embellished stucco decorations and gilt furniture with red silk upholstery. An example of this ostentatious style can now be seen at the Louvre in the apartments of Napoleon III, which were occupied by the Ministry of Finance from 1871 to 1989.

The Galerie d'Apollon, the jewel of the Department of Decorative Arts, houses the Crown jewels, most notably the 140-carat *Regent* diamond. Purchased by the Regent in 1717, it adorned the crowns of Louis XV, Louis XVI, and Charles X, as well as the hilt of Napoleon's sword and Empress Eugénie's diadem.

Following page

Equestrian Statuette of Charlemagne

Carolingian art, 9th century / Bronze with gilt traces.

This bronze work from the Cathedral of Metz is the only Carolingian statuette that has come down to the present.

Thousands of objets d'art...

WHEN THE PERIOD OF ANTIQUITY CAME TO A CLOSE and the Medieval world emerged around the 5th century, the production of arts and crafts objects was at first greatly inspired by the Graeco-Roman tradition. When Neoclassicism became popular during the reign of Napoleon I, artists returned once more to the ideals of Antiquity. Throughout its history, the Western world has regularly turned to Antiquity in its search for new forms.

THE HISTORY OF TASTE is made up of the absorption of different—and sometimes contradictory—elements. Styles from the distant past may thus play a part in the emergence of new forms of expression.

DURING THE REIGN OF LOUIS XIV, Renaissance sobriety and a return to Antiquity combined with the dynamism of Italian Baroque to develop French Neoclassicism, which came to represent elegance and grandeur.

SUCH SUBTLE ALCHEMY resulted in a coherent style touching on all media, as is amply illustrated by the examples of decorative art in the Louvre. The interlocking curves and swirls of the Rococo style developed early in the 18th century; its reed and shell forms and floral motifs would be found over and over again, whether on a desk by a cabinetmaker from the Faubourg Saint-Antoine such as Jacques Dubois, on a porcelain clock from a Strasbourg factory, or on a silver gilt *Chocolate-Maker* designed by the Parisian silversmith Henri-Nicolas Cousinet for Queen Maria Leczinska. The same motifs decorate the façade of the Hôtel de Lassay in Paris, and the friezes of the Hôtel de Soubise, which now houses the Archives Nationales. They are also apparent in the paintings of Natoire and Boucher.

COMPARING THE COVER of the novel *The Hunchback of Notre Dame* with the motifs on a stock certificate issued by the water board, Marcel Proust wrote: 'Everything belonging to the same epoch looks alike.' Time rubs out the differences that may have made plastic, graphic, and intellectual forms of expression seem so unlike one another to their contemporaries. And that no doubt is what is known as a style.

LÉONARD LIMOSIN

**Portrait of the Connétable
de Montmorency**

1556 / Enamel on copper and gilt wood.

Léonard Limosin, enameller to François I,
painted this portrait of the High Constable of France,
embellished with ornaments characteristic
of the School of Fontainebleau.

SIXTH PIECE IN THE SET OF TAPESTRIES
known as 'MAXIMILIAN'S HUNT' AFTER BERNARD VAN ORLEY

December

Circa 1528-1533 / Silk and wool tapestry, with gold-and-silver thread.

This piece is part of a set of twelve tapestries, each representing a month of the year, woven after drawings by Bernard van Orley
and inspired by Gaston Phébus' *Livre de la Chasse*. The set was bequeathed by Mazarin to Louis XIV and restored in 1733.

ANDRÉ-CHARLES BOULLE

Wardrobe

Circa 1700 / Oak, with ebony and tortoiseshell veneering, and brass, tin, tinted horn, coloured wood, and gilt bronze marquetry.

From 1672, André-Charles Boulle, cabinetmaker, had workshops at the Louvre in which he produced beautiful furniture for the king and other connoisseurs. Although Boulle did not invent the marquetry technique to which he gave his name, he was its leading exponent.

HENRI-NICOLAS COUSINET

Chocolate-Maker and Heater

1729-1730 / Silver gilt, ebony.

This chocolate-maker belonging to Queen Maria Leczinska, wife of Louis XV,
was made when the Dauphin was born in 1729.

ROYAL PORCELAIN FACTORY, SÈVRES

Chinese Breakfast Set Belonging to Queen Marie-Amélie

1840 / Porcelain

Queen Marie-Amélie, wife of Louis-Philippe, liked the elegance and exoticism of the designs created
by the Royal Porcelain Factory of Sèvres. Thanks to numerous royal orders, the factory flourished.

The main salon of Napoleon III's apartments at the Louvre

Occupied until 1989 by the Ministry of Finance, the main reception salon of Napoleon III's apartments
is lavishly decorated with burgundy velvet upholstery, gilt, mirrors, and crystal chandeliers.
This ostentatious style dominated Napoleon III's reign.

The Galerie d'Apollon

IN OCTOBER 1850, a few months after he was commissioned to paint the ceiling of the Galerie d'Apollon, Eugène Delacroix wrote to one of his friends: 'It's a major work that will be located in one of the most beautiful places in the world, next to Le Brun's superb compositions. As you can see, it will be easy to fall short, and I will have to keep a steady course.' In August 1851, Delacroix's painting, *Apollo Defeating the Serpent Python,* was installed in the central ceiling area, thus completing the decorations begun by Louis XIV's painter. Today, the gallery is known both for its luxurious ornamentation, executed by two masters of painting who seem to be in competition with each other, and for its magnificent displays: the Louvre's collection of royal treasures, including some of the Crown diamonds.

WHEN THE SECOND EMPIRE FELL, the State took over its possessions, which included 51,403 diamonds cut as brilliants, 21,119 rose diamonds, 2,962 pearls, 507 rubies, 136 sapphires, 250 emeralds, 528 turquoises, 22 opals, 235 amethysts, and about 500 other precious stones. Part of the royal treasure is exhibited in the Galerie d'Apollon for its artistic and historical interest. Some works are in the Natural History Museum, while others were melted down (including the imperial crown). Many jewels were sold off at nine public auctions, held between May 12 and 23, 1887. Among the satisfied buyers were jewellers Tiffany's of New York and Boucheron of Paris.

The income from the sales totalled 6,927,509 francs in gold.

AUGUSTIN DUFLOS
after the design of
CLAUDE RONDÉ

Louis XV's Crown

1722

At Louis XV's coronation, the *Regent*, a famous
140-carat diamond belonging to Philippe d'Orléans,
Regent of France before the king came of age,
was prominently displayed in this crown.

ORIENTAL ANTIQUITIES

• Richelieu Wing
Mesopotamia, Ancient Iran   Ground Floor
Islamic Art   Mezzanine
Temporary Exhibitions   Mezzanine

• Sully Wing
Countries of the Levant   Ground Floor

EGYPTIAN ANTIQUITIES

• Sully Wing
Entrance (Crypt of the Sphinx)   Mezzanine
Pharaonic Egypt   Ground Floor
                                                    First Floor
Christian Egypt (Coptic Art)   Ground Floor

GREEK, ETRUSCAN, AND ROMAN ANTIQUITIES

• Denon Wing
Greek Antiquities   Ground Floor
Etruscan Antiquities   Ground Floor

• Sully Wing
Roman Antiquities   Ground Floor
Bronzes and Precious Objects   First Floor
Ceramics and Terracottas   First Floor

DECORATIVE ARTS (OBJETS D'ART)

• Richelieu Wing
Middle Ages, Renaissance   First Floor
19th century: First Empire   First Floor
Napoleon III's Apartments   First Floor
Research Area   First Floor
Temporary Exhibitions   Mezzanine

• Sully Wing
17th-18th centuries   First Floor
19th century: Restoration, July Monarchy   First Floor

• Denon Wing
Galerie d'Apollon (Crown Jewels)   First Floor

SCULPTURE

• Richelieu Wing
French Sculpture: Middle Ages, Renaissance   Ground Floor
17th-19th centuries   Mezzanine
                                                    Ground Floor
Temporary Exhibitions   Mezzanine

• Denon Wing
Italian Sculpture: 11th-15th centuries   Mezzanine
16th-19th centuries   Ground Floor
Northern European Sculpture: 12th-16th centuries   Mezzanine
17th-19th centuries   Ground Floor

PAINTINGS

• Richelieu Wing
Northern Schools of Painting:
Netherlands, Flanders, Germany   Second Floor
French Paintings: 14th-17th centuries   Second Floor

• Sully Wing
French Paintings: 17th-19th centuries   Second Floor

• Denon Wing
French Paintings: 19th century (large works)   First Floor
Italian Paintings   First Floor
Spanish Paintings   First Floor
Temporary Exhibitions   Second Floor

PRINTS AND DRAWINGS

• Richelieu Wing
Northern European Schools   Second Floor

• Sully Wing
French School   Second Floor
Temporary Exhibitions   First Floor

• Denon Wing
Italian School   First Floor
Temporary Exhibitions   Second Floor
Research Area   First Floor
(1 p.m.-6 p.m., Monday through Friday)
Consulting Room   First Floor
(with previous permission only)
E. de Rothschild Collection   First Floor
(by appointment only)

THE MEDIEVAL LOUVRE HISTORY OF THE LOUVRE

• Sully Wing   Mezzanine

RICHELIEU

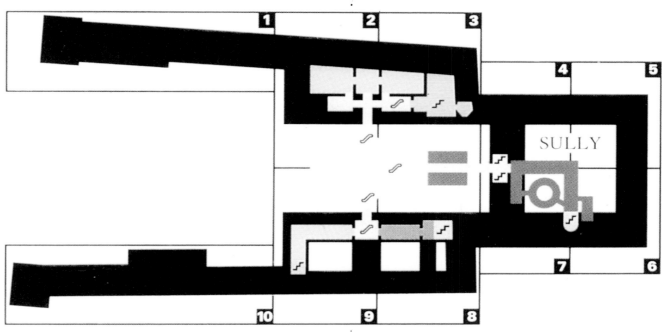

DENON

Oriental Antiquities		Sculpture		Northern European Sculpture		Temporary	
Islamic Art	**3**	French Sculpture:		12th-16th centuries	**9**	Exhibitions	**2**
Information	**3**	Information	**2**	**The Medieval Louvre**	**7**		
Egyptian Antiquities		17th-18th centuries	**2 3**	**History of the Louvre**	**3 8**		
Access (Crypt of the Sphinx	**6**	Italian Sculpture:		Paintings, sculptures, scale			
Pharaonic Egypt	**7**	11th-15th centuries	**9**	models			

Ground Floor

Oriental Antiquities		Greek, Etruscan, and Roman		Sculpture		Northern European Sculpture:	
Information	**3**	**Antiquities**		French Sculpture:		17th-19th centuries	**9**
Mesopotamia, Ancient Iran	**3 4**	Salle du Manège (copies)	**9**	Middle Ages, Renaissance	**2**	(Michelangelo's *Slaves*)	**9**
Egyptian Antiquities		Greek Antiquities	**7 8**	17th-19th centuries	**2 3**		
Pharaonic Egypt	**6**	Etruscan Antiquities	**8**	Italian Sculpture:			
Christian Egypt	**6**	Roman Antiquities	**8**	16th-19th centuries	**9**		
(The Seated Scribe)	**6**	*(The Venus de Milo)*	**7**				

RICHELIEU

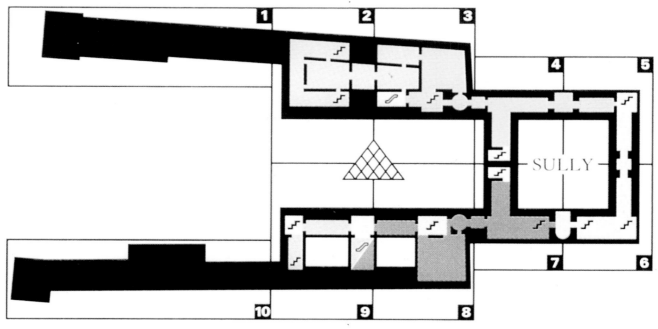

DENON

RICHELIEU

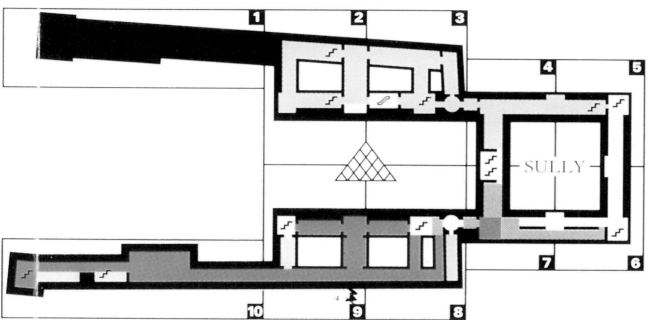

DENON

Egyptian Antiquities	**Decorative Arts**	Galerie d'Apollon **8**	Spanish Paintings **10**
Pharaonic Egypt **6 7**	Middle Ages, Renaissance **2 3**	(Crown Jewels)	**Decorative Arts**
Greek, Etruscan,	17th-18th centuries **3 4 5**	**Paintings**	Italian School **9**
and Roman Antiquities	First Empire **2**	French Paintings:	Research Area **10**
Bronzes and Precious Objects **7**	Restoration, July Monarchy **4**	19th century **8 9**	Consulting Room **10**
Ceramics, terracottas **7**	Napoleon III's Apartments **2**	Italian Paintings **8 9 10**	E. de Rothschild Collection **10**
	Research Area **2**	(Mona Lisa) **8**	Temporary Exhibitions **7**

Paintings	**Northern European Paintings:**	**Prints and Drawings**
French Paintings:	Netherlands, Flander **2 3**	French School:
14th-17th centuries **3 4 5**	Germany **2 3**	17th century **4**
18th-19th centuries **5 6 7**	V. Lyon and De Croy	18th century **5 6**
Information Room **3**	Collections **7**	Northern European Schools **3**
		Temporary Exhibitions **10**

RICHELIEU

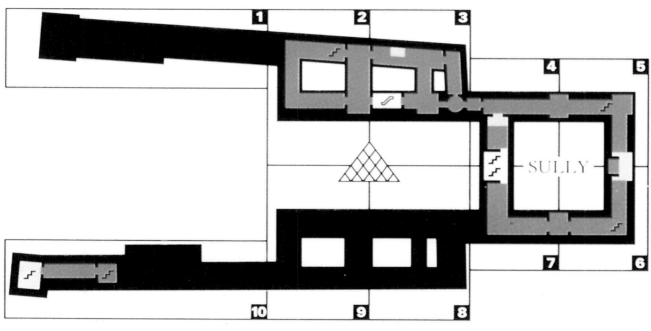

DENON

Bibliography and Photographic Credits

BRESC GENEVIÈVE, *Mémoires du Louvre*, Paris, Gallimard, 1989.

CALLU AGNÈS, *Réunion des Musées nationaux, 1870-1940*, Paris, école des Chartes, 1994.

GALARD JEAN, *Visiteurs du Louvre*, Paris, Réunion des Musées nationaux, 1993.

HAUTECŒUR LOUIS, *Histoire du Louvre, Le château, le palais, le musée, des origines à nos jours, 1200-1940*, Paris, L'Illustration, s.d.

HOOG SIMONE, *Le Bernin, Louis XIV, une statue « déplacée »*, Paris Adam Biro, 1989.

LOBRICHON GUY, *L'Histoire de Paris par la peinture*, Paris, Belfond, 1988.

PEÏ IEOH MING et BASIANI ÉMILE, *Les Grands desseins du Louvre*, Paris Hemann, 1989.

QUONIAM PIERRE et GUINAMARD LAURENT, *Le Palais du Louvre*, Paris, Nathan, 1988.

RAGER CATHERINE, *Pikto-Louvre*, Paris, Adam Biro, 1990.

SCHNEIDER PIERRE, *Les Dialogues du Louvre*, Paris, Adam Biro, 1991.

WORKS BY SEVERAL AUTHORS

– *Le louvre, Trésors du plus grand musée du monde*, Paris, Sélection du Reader's Digest, 1991.

– *Louvre, Guide des collections*, Paris, Réunion des Musées nationaux, 1989.

– *Guide du visiteur : les Antiquités orientales*, Paris, Réunion des Musées nationaux, 1993.

– *Guide du visiteur : Les Arts de l'islam*, Paris, Réunion des Musées nationaux, 1993.

– *Guide du visiteur : Les Objets d'art*, Paris, Réunion des Musées nationaux, 1993.

– *Guide du visiteur : La Peinture française*, Paris, Réunion des Musées nationaux, 1993.

– *Guide du visiteur : La Peinture flamande, hollandaise et allemande*, Paris, Réunion des Musées nationaux, 1993.

– *Guide du visiteur : La Sculpture française*, Paris, Réunion des Musées nationaux, 1993.

Information Desk

9 a.m. to 9.45 p.m.; closed Tuesdays. Tel.: 33.1.40.20.53.17. Free map in six languages.

Free Cloakroom and Baggage Room

All belongings deposited in the cloakroom must be collected the same day.

Cash, chequebooks, credit cards, valuables, fur coats, food, and drinks are not accepted.

An area for changing babies is provided for your convenience; strollers are available upon request at the Information Desk. Lost and Found: 33.1.40.20.53.17.

Group Visits

Daily, except Sunday afternoons after 1 p.m., first Sunday of each month, Tuesdays, and public holidays. Groups are allowed to visit Napoleon III's Apartments only before 3 p.m. Entry through the Passage Richelieu or the Galerie du Carrousel, after 6 p.m. through the Pyramid. Advanced booking required at the following numbers: Groups accompanied by their own guide: Tel. 33.1.40.20.57.60. Fax 33.1.40.20.58.24.

To make an appointment for a guided visit with a museum lecturer: Tel. 33.1.40.20.51.77. Fax 33.1.40.20.54.46. Groups consist of seven to thirty visitors (twenty in the Department of Decorative Arts).

For reservations, rates and specific services, please consult the information brochure at the Group Information Desk ('Accueil des Groupes'). The museum's multimedia library provides free information (by post on request) to school and group leaders wishing to prepare a visit: Tel. 33.1.40.20.52.80.

Disabled Visitors

Tel. 33.1.40.20.59.90.

An orientation guide in French or English is available at the Information Desk. Nearly all of the Richelieu Wing is accessible to visitors in wheelchairs. Lifts and special equipment are available at several points in the Denon and Sully wings. For blind and partially sighted visitors, the Department of Sculpture has opened a gallery housing about twenty works that may be touched while listening to explanations on an audioguide. Guided visits may be booked for disabled groups or for sight-impaired visitors: Tel. 33.1.40.20.54.32 and 33.1.40.20.58.76. Guided visits for the hearing impaired are also available: 33.1.40.20.44.81. Loan of wheelchairs upon request: Tel. 33.1.40.20.53.17.

Rules for Visitors

Please refrain from using flashes on cameras. Visitors are not allowed to bring cumbersome objects, animals, or food into the galleries. Smoking, eating, and drinking are also prohibited. The museum's regulation book for visitors may be consulted at the Information Desk.

Bookshop, Shops, and Chalcography

From 9.30 a.m. to 9.45 p.m., guidebooks, art books, reproductions, engravings, postcards, films about the Louvre, gift items, jewellery, and casts: Tel. 33.1.40.20.52.06.

Restaurants and cafés

• Under the Pyramid, from 9 a.m. to 9.45 p.m.:
Le Grand Louvre (gastronomic restaurant): tel. 33.1.40.20.53.41 (till midnight),
Le Café du Louvre, Le Café Napoléon, and *La Cafétéria.*
• Inside the museum: *Le Café Mollien* (Denon Wing, 1st floor) and *Le Café Richelieu* (Richelieu Wing, 1st floor).
• Entrance from the outside, Richelieu side: *Le Café Marly,* from 8 a.m. to 2 a.m.

Information Screens

Video screens in the Hall Napoleon provide daily information on the rooms that may be visited and on the museum's activities.

Information is also available by Minitel (36 15) Louvre or by telephone: 33.1.40.20.53.17, from 9 a.m. to 9.45 p.m. Wednesday-Monday.

Audioguides

Available in six languages at the Richelieu, Sully, and Denon entrances on the mezzanine level.
Temporary Exhibitions
• In the permanent collections, at the usual museum rates and opening hours.
• Under the Pyramid, from 10 a.m. to 9.15 p.m., special rate.

Guided Visits, Workshop Activities

Tickets and meeting point at the Group Desk ('Accueil des Groupes')
Detailed brochures at the Information Desk.
Individual Visitors
• General or specialised tours (some in English) are regularly scheduled: Tel. 33.1.40.20.52.09.
• Workshops for children, teenagers, adults: Tel. 33.1.40.20.52.63.

Auditorium (420 seats)

Lectures, conferences, concerts, films.
Information, reservations, season tickets: Tel. 33.1.40.20.52.99.

Films about the Louvre

Films produced by the Louvre are screened daily from 10 a.m. in the audiovisual room under the Pyramid, near the Information Desk. Free of charge.
Address
• Musée du Louvre, 75058 Paris Cedex 01. Tel. 33.1.40.20.50.50.
• General Information:
Recorded information service: 33.1.40.20.51.51. Minitel: 36 15 Louvre. Internet: http://www.louvre.fr/
Information and reception: 33.1.40.20.53.17.
Main entrance through the Pyramid.

How to get to the Louvre

• Metro: Palais-Royal/Musée du Louvre
• Bus: 21, 27, 39, 48, 68, 69, 72, 81, 95.
• Underground car park: Avenue du Général-Lemonnier, daily from 7 a.m. to 11 p.m. Tel 33.1.42.44.16.32.
• Through the Galerie du Carrousel (entrance through the Carrousel Garden, or at 99 Avenue de Rivoli). Tel. 33.1.43.16.47.47.

Museum Opening Hours

Every day except Tuesdays and some public holidays:
Permanent collections: 9 a.m. to 6 p.m.; evening hours to 9.45 p.m. on Mondays (some rooms only) and Wednesdays (the entire museum). Galleries start closing at 5.30 p.m. or 9.30 p.m.
Medieval Louvre and History of the Louvre: 9 a.m. to 9.45 p.m.
Temporary exhibitions under the Pyramid: 10 a.m. to 9.45 p.m.

Tickets

Reduced rates for everyone after 3 p.m. and on Sundays. Free for under those under 18. Tickets valid all day, re-entry allowed. Sale of tickets ends at 5.15 p.m. or at 9.15 p.m.

Free entry on the first Sunday of every month.
Museum-and-Monument Pass

Valid for one, three, or five days. Provides entry to 65 museums and monuments, including the permanent collections of the Louvre. On sale under the Pyramid and at the Carrousel du Louvre. Information: Tel. 33.1.44.78.45.81.

Annual Pass

Provides free entry to the permanent collections and temporary exhibitions. Price: from 300 F annually.
Information and membership: under the Pyramid, at the Société des Amis du Louvre. Tel. 33.1.40.20.53.74.